NTARIA

Cairns

· Mt. Isa

Sydney ·

Old Coast Wer

Van Diemen Inlet
Point Burrowes

Point Austin

Tidal flats

Bloo

Station Creek

Crooked C

Accident Inlet
Fitzmaurice Point

Brannigan C

Pilot Station
Alligator Point
⚓ Karumba

Walker

NORMAN

BYNOE

Tidal flats

RIVER

Wills Creek

ore Point

*saster
Inlet*

Middle Point

Morning Inlet

Spring

FLINDERS

Saltwater Creek

Tools Lagoon Creek

Norm

Goose

Tidal flats

Alligator Lagoon

· *Teeswater Lake*

RIVER

Magowra

Magowra C

Rocky
Lake

Rock Creek

Manrika Lake

Tidal flats

Catherine C

Armstrong

Twelve Mile
Lagoon

Buffalo Lake

ondamus Creek

C Creek

Creek

"*Plain Creek*"

Larr

· Old Punchbowl Yard

THE SWEETNESS OF THE FIG

Aboriginal Women in Transition

The SWEETNESS of the FIG

ABORIGINAL WOMEN IN TRANSITION

Virginia Huffer

with the collaboration of Elsie Roughsey
and other women of Mornington Island

New South Wales University Press   Sydney

University of Washington Press   Seattle and London

Published jointly by the
New South Wales University Press Limited
Box 1, P.O., Kensington, N.S.W., Australia 2033
and the
University of Washington Press
Seattle, Washington 98105

Printed by Southwood Press Pty Ltd, Sydney, Australia

National Library of Australia Card Number 0 86840-152-8

Library of Congress Cataloging in Publication Data
Huffer, Virginia.

  The sweetness of the fig.
  Bibliography: p. x + 166.
  1. Women, Australian (Aboriginal) — Australia-Mornington Island.
  2. Roughsey, Elsie.
  3. Australian aborigines — Biography.
  4. Mornington Island, Australia — Social conditions.
  I. Roughsey, Elsie, joint author.
  II. Title.
  GN667.Q4H83   305.4'8   80-21658
ISBN 0-295-95790-5 (UWP)

Contents

ELSIE ROUGHSEY

'I have nothing to be ashamed of and you have written about my life as I have known and lived it. I want the world to know what life is like on Mornington Island. If any student can learn anything from it, I will be pleased.'

Elsie Roughsey

Acknowledgements

This modest book would not have been possible without the marked interest, frequent discussions and critical reading of the several drafts of the manuscript by Dr John Cawte, of the School of Psychiatry, University of New South Wales. I am deeply grateful to him for all of this, and even more for his friendship.

I am indebted to Dr Eugene B. Brody, Chairman of the Department of Psychiatry, University of Maryland School of Medicine, for his encouragement, his reading and useful comments concerning the content of the manuscript. In addition, many thanks to Professor Leslie Kiloh, Head of the School of Psychiatry, University of New South Wales, for his gracious hospitality in providing me with the resources of his department.

I am grateful to the Australian Institute of Aboriginal Studies in Canberra, Australia, for their financial support which contributed to making this study of Aboriginal women possible, as well as to the University of Maryland School of Medicine for permitting me to have sabbatical leave to take a fascinating journey to the other side of the world and to learn to know the people of Australia, both the Aborigines and the Europeans.

Several colleagues and friends have read the material concerning the Aboriginal women of Mornington Island and have offered helpful comments. These include Dr Nancy Waxler, who made a brief trip to the island with me, and my lifelong friend, the author Elizabeth Harrover Johnson, and my colleague, Dr James Mackie. I want to especially acknowledge the most valuable assistance given by my associate, Dr Eleanore Jantz. In addition to making very useful suggestions for organization, she carefully read and helped to edit the final revision. I am appreciative of the patience of my secretaries, Frances Knott and Judy Lubao, who typed the various drafts.

Especial thanks are due to the Rev. and Mrs Douglas Belcher, Mr A. M. Gibson, and the entire Mornington Island Presbyterian Mission staff for their help and hospitality. It was a great opportunity and pleasure to learn to know Elsie Roughsey and the other women of Mornington Island — I am indeed appreciative of their co-operation and friendship.

1
The Nature of the Study

Aboriginal women living with their families on an isolated island in Australia provide the focus of this study. The material presented is essentially the life-history of one woman, with vignettes from the lives of about twenty others. The Australian Aborigines share the problems of other excluded peoples; however, the wishes, ideals, and the difficulties of this group of women are similar to those of many Western women. They want better housing for themselves, and better education and job opportunities for their children. The middle-aged mothers tend to be deeply concerned about the irresponsible behaviour and lack of motivation shown by the younger generation.

At the same time, these women continue to maintain the beliefs and customs of traditional Aboriginal culture. Sorcery and other forms of magic continue to influence their thinking. Kinship rules and relationships, although fragmented, survive as an important feature of their society. As their stories unfold, it will be evident that the Mornington Island Aborigines are truly transitional figures. Part of their psychological, social and cultural life reflects the heritage from their forebears in the dim past, while in a number of ways they are markedly Westernized.

The Sweetness of the Fig concerns Aboriginal women as they live in the latter third of the twentieth century. The focus is not on psychopathology, but on the life-story, with special emphasis on psychological and social aspects of selected Aboriginal women in a particular community with its own unique culture. Through biographical sketches of the women, the integrated qualities of their personalities and their adaption to their environment, as well as their potential for social change, are revealed.

Areas of attention include the early psychological and cultural influences in their lives, their socialization, and their current position in their community as women, wives, and mothers. How do they spend their time? What do they see as their frustrations, their pleasures, their hopes, and how do they adjust to the problems of living? How will they adapt to any future changes in their society, especially if imposed from outside (from greater Australia)? Some of these questions will be answered as aspects of their life-histories are related.

The use of personal life-histories has been one of the main methods used in the development of personality theory, especially psychoanalytic. The classic instances include Freud's case histories.[1] The sociologist has used the personal document to a much less extent; he has been more interested in 'cold hard facts', and for the most part has not sought the help that this method can give in probing the subtleties of the human condition.[2]

In contrast to the position of the sociologist, Kluckhohn in 1945 emphasized the importance of life-histories in anthropological research, asserting that the 'subjective factor' in the lives of human groups is a problem of crucial importance.[3] It was at that time that the controversies over 'nature versus nurture' and 'culture versus personality' were being argued. Kardiner, in an influential book in this area, stated, 'The concept of culture becomes an operational tool, when implemented by the psychological insight into the knowledge that different practices of living are created by different problems of adaption, and that these practices have specific influence on the individual if integrated during the process of growth.'[4]

More recently, Langness emphasized the demand for personality data in depth, as well as for more reliable cultural data.[5] He pointed out that there is no substitute in transcultural research for the life-history in whict the emphasis is on internalization and motivation. Hughes has stated that 'the central goal of life-history research is to examine patterns of personality functioning in relation to life circumstances'.[6] He also made the point that biographical materials help in obtaining an understanding of the nature of nonpathology as well as 'sickness'.

There have been intensive studies of Australian Aboriginal society and culture, but there has been relative neglect of the personal life-history. There have been several biographical or autobiographical publications concerning Aboriginal men who have become public figures.[7] In addition, there have been personal tributes involving the life-histories of two Aboriginal men by anthropologists whom they befriended.[8] Recently an autobiography has been published by Dick Roughsey, a native of Mornington Island and the husband of my collaborator, Elsie Roughsey.

There have been few reports of the intimate and detailed life of the Aboriginal woman. This can be explained in several ways. Marie Reay said that Aboriginal women were in general socially subservient to men, and were to a great extent excluded from knowledge of the spiritual world and performance of sacred rites.[10] Apparently, therefore, they were not sought out by field workers as a source of information concerning the Aboriginal view of the world. Reay claimed that male anthropologists gained only a sketchy impression of the female activities because of their limited transactions and rapport with the women. Catherine Berndt stated that 'the position of Aboriginal women clearly needs to be seen in more impartial perspective than has been the case in the past'.[11]

Phyllis Kaberry in 1939 published an important book that dealt with the Aboriginal women in the Kimberley District of north-west Australia.[12] In it she examined the women's economic and ceremonial life, their spiritual beliefs, their transition from childhood to maturity, and their marital life. In 1951 Catherine Berndt, in collaboration with her husband, wrote a monograph in which they showed how marriage and sexual life were an expression of a particular cultural pattern.[13] During a symposium, a number of anthropologists reported on various aspects of woman's role in Aboriginal society.[14] Jane Goodale used the life-cycle of the women of Melville Island, Australia, as a frame of reference to discuss many aspects of Tiwi culture.[15]

Upon consideration of the above factors, it seemed desirable to supplement the ethnopsychiatric research currently being conducted in Australia, especially by the psychiatric field team of the University of New South Wales under the direction of Dr John Cawte.[16] In view of the paucity of studies of Aboriginal women, and with the value of the life-histories in mind, the project reported here was undertaken.

For those readers who have little knowledge of the origins, social structure, way of life, and traditions of the Australian Aborigine, a résumé is given. This book is not intended to be a detailed anthropological presentation. However, more specific information about the customs, rituals, and beliefs of the particular people studied will be related in subsequent chapters in order to enable some understanding of how aspects of their heritage are interwoven into their current life-style and how these may influence their future adjustment.

It is estimated that Aborigines have inhabited the isolated subcontinent of Australia for more than 30 000 years.[17] Their origin is obscure; possibly they migrated from south-east Asia. Similarities in hair distribution and certain bony-skull features have been considered indications that the Aborigines are proto-caucasoids. However, among the various tribes there is enough dissimilarity in blood groupings and fingerprint patterns to discredit the idea of a common genetic pool. These so-called Australoids were essentially cut off from modernity by geographical isolation and ocean currents until the Europeans began arriving as settlers in the late eighteenth century.

The vast subcontinent which the Aborigines inhabited provided a harsh environment, with extremes of climate and rainfall. Australia had no animals suitable for herding, nor plants for cultivation. The indigenous people lived by food gathering, hunting and fishing. Their survival depended upon finding fresh water. A social system evolved that was adapted to the hunter-gatherer way of life, which might be confined to an area of adequate water supply, or might require moving about from waterhole to waterhole.

The Aboriginal culture was marked by a deliberate limitation of material possessions. A man might carry a spear, a boomerang, and perhaps a spear-thrower; a woman usually had a digging stick and a bowl-like receptacle — all of wood. They made no pottery; built no permanent homes, merely windbreaks or brush shelters; and in the hotter climates they went about naked. Possession of property was incompatible with a nomadic existence.

In contrast to the simplicity of their material life — represented by their rejection of property — was their development of an elaborately organized social, conceptual, and ritual world. Each group had its own country (area) where its ancestors were believed to sojourn as pre-existing spirits waiting for reincarnation. The group consisted not only of human beings but also of several other species (totems); all were relations. In their cermonial life, forms of artistic expression achieved high prominence and portrayed the relation of man to his Ancestral Beings and to Nature, unlimited by space and time.

Illness was attributed to sorcery, and death could only be prevented by the medicine man ('clever fellow'). The indigenous Australian had a highly developed kinship system, which regulated behaviour and marriage rules.

It has been estimated that when the European settlers first arrived, there were living in Australia about 300 000 Aborigines, divided into approximately 500 tribes.[18] The impact was catastrophic for the Aborigines: their best lands were appropriated, their diet deteriorated, and they succumbed to introduced pathogens such as smallpox virus. The settlers employed them to a certain extent as labourers. Some Aborigines gave up nomadic life to live in shanty settlements in order to acquire some of the material things the white man had. Tribal life and institutions became less important to them, especially with the advent of Mission or government schools. White male settlers cohabited with Aboriginal women, producing many offspring of mixed ancestry. The ranks of the full-blooded Aborigines declined so that by 1960 only 45 000 were thought to survive. More recently, with better health care and diet, the number of both full-blooded and mixed-blooded Aborigines has been increasing, and increasing rapidly.

At present few Aborigines continue to live a nomadic life. Currently there are five environmental groupings of Aborigines:
1. urban dwellers;
2. fringe groups on the outskirts of country towns;
3. rural workers on pastoral (sheep or cattle) properties;
4. those living on Reseryes, under government or Mission supervision; and
5. small autonomous communities which have 'hived off' from settlements in order to live a more traditional life in remote outstations.

The Biographical Subjects and Method
The place selected for my study of Aboriginal women was Mornington Island, in the Gulf of Carpentaria, Queensland. This island is a Mission reserve under the direction of the Mission Board of the Presbyterian Church of Australia. At the time of my first trip to Mornington Island in 1970, my introduction to the Aborigines and the Mission staff was facilitated by the fact that my Australian colleague, Dr John Cawte, was known to most of the people.

The Missionary, the Reverend Douglas Belcher M.B.E., had told several of the leading men of the village that a woman doctor was coming and was going to be especially interested in talking with the women, and probably with one woman extensively. No selection had been made as to which woman would be the subject of the life-history, although the two Lardil men who were appointed to greet me on my arrival had a somewhat elderly, dignified woman with them, as if they had preselected her.

During the first week, I spent each morning sitting on a blanket on the ground by the house of one of my male greeters, Dick Roughsey, His wife; Elsie, served as my unofficial hostess. Other women, usually aged over forty, were invited to stop by to 'yarn' (a colloquial expression, both Aboriginal and Australian, which means to have a long comfortable chat). These women, two to five in number at any one time, were of the Lardil tribe and had a fair-to-good command of English. Initially, some had difficulty in understanding my American accent, but that was usually quickly remedied by another 'translating' for me into Australian. Their ability to relate comfortably, spontaneously and with some degree of introspection was highly variable. I explained to them that a number of men had visited their island to study their 'old ways', their language and customs, and their health, but none of the previous investigators had talked very much with the women, and that I wanted to get to know them as one woman to another. I said that I was interested in their everyday life, their problems and pleasures. I also wanted to learn about their beliefs and practices which they had inherited from the time before the missionaries arrived.

During the first ten days, three activities were spontaneously agreed on for 'us women': a corroboree with only female dancers, a fishing trip to the next island, and an expedition to gather rock oysters. From this, it would seem that a level of rapport and acceptance had been established rather rapidly. The only indication of a negative attitude towards me was revealed during the first few days when several casual references were made to the murder of the first missionary, the Reverend Robert Hall, by an Aborigine.

Beginning with the initial contact I made copious notes, usually verbatim, during the entire time spent with the women. This practice seemed acceptable, probably because other investigators had done likewise. A tape recorder was not used because I feared it would inhibit freedom of talk during the interview, or at least distract my own attention. The only time that note-taking was temporarily suspended was when one or all seemed embarrassed in talking about sexual matters. My own questions, answers, or subjective responses were also recorded.

The group meetings were useful in obtaining an overall view of the life of the women and their interactions. However, it soon became evident that individual sessions would probably be more productive. In addition to being poor informants, their social inhibitions prevented some of the women from discussing personal matters such as birth control. I was especially interested in obtaining information concerning their knowledge of and attitudes toward contraception.

My unofficial hostess, Elsie Roughsey, soon revealed her superior ability to talk spontaneously, almost in a free associative manner. Her knowledge of the traditional culture, her openness concerning her worries and experiences, and her naturalness in revealing her own character made her a good subject for obtaining a detailed life-history. An interviewer is aware that, to some degree, any informant is naturally going to report only what he or she wants to tell, or thinks the interviewer wants to hear. However, Elsie seemed remarkably non-defensive. She was agreeable to meeting alone with me for three or four hours each day. In this way she was seen for approximately seventy-five hours. With the previous group contact and other social interaction, we related to each other for about 125 hours during my first visit to the island. No mention was made of any remuneration for the time spent, until the night before my departure, when I suggested with a gift of cash or of articles that she might want that were not obtainable on the island. Elsie chose the latter.

While Elsie was the principal subject of my study, it seemed important to learn to know some of the other women in this particular village. The fallacy of generalizing from one informant in drawing any conclusions about a social group is obvious, just as is the fallacy of generalizing from the findings in one tribe of Aborigines to another. While there may be many characteristics in common, especially if individuals live in an isolated community such as Mornington Island, each person has his own personality, problems, hopes, and attitudes. Life-styles and repertoires of coping with the exigencies of living may be highly variable. For this reason a number of other women in the village were interviewed, and the material presented concerning them points up this variability.

Depending upon factors such as their ability to relate to me, the type of situation they presented, and their own interest in or willingness for further meetings, one to three interviews of approximately ninety minutes each were held with the women, usually in individual sessions. Frequently these women were also seen in various other situations around the village. Several had been part of the original group that met together in Elsie's front yard during my early days on the island.

Those interviewed varied in age from fifteen to about sixty-five years. The different tribal backgrounds were included: Lardil, Kaiadilt, those born on the mainland of Australia and brought to the island as children, and those who more recently had come to the island as a result of marriage. In arranging for an interview, I asked whether they preferred to come to the house in the Mission area where I was lodged, or for me to come to their house, or to meet elsewhere in the village such as under the trees behind the hospital. The choice usually reflected the social distance that they felt either between themselves and the Mission, or with me. At other times, it was determined by the presence of young children at home who needed some supervision. No remuneration was offered to any in this group, although occasionally they were given a package of biscuits or dried fruit for their children after the interview was concluded.

Obviously, only those who would agree to interviews were seen. In general, most of the women were both willing and cooperative; however, several consented only reluctantly. Some of those approached declined to be informants or failed to keep their appointments; these were primarily women in their early twenties.

Prior to my return to the island in 1973, I wrote to Elsie and to each of the other women saying that I was planning a trip to Mornington

Island and was looking forward to talking with them again. There was quite a difference in attitudes expressed during my second visit. The majority of the women greeted me like an old friend. Those who had been avoidant were pleased to talk with me and were relatively spontaneous in their communications. When asked about their previous reluctance, the reply was, 'I was shy'.

The Problem of Anonymity
My first visit to Mornington Island was made with the object of conducting a psychobiographical study of at least one Aboriginal woman, or at least to assay the difficulties and constraints that might affect this procedure. I made copious notes while talking with the informants. Elsie Roughsey, who later became my collaborator, was aware of my intention to publish the material. Her husband, Dick, expected that his own book, *Moon and Rainbow,*[19] would be released very soon. It may not have been implicit to most of the other women that I was hoping to publish a study using the information they gave me. Only one woman asked me if real or false names would be used in a publication; she was told that false names would be substituted.

However, after leaving the island, I became concerned about the anonymity — or lack of it — of my informants. This raised several problems. As a psychiatrist, I am accustomed to hearing intimacies and to maintaining confidentiality in publication of clinical material. Disguising the data given by the Mornington Island women would have impaired its validity. It was not advisable to falsify the locale, to identify it as an arid zone, or make it a government reserve, since that would have resulted in socio-cultural distortions.

But even more important to me was my fear of betraying the women who had freely given me their personal experiences and feelings. It is one thing for an informant to tell an investigator intimate experiences and to see the information being recorded, but reading it in print can certainly evoke a different response. If the women were to read the material, each could not only identify herself, but also most of the others. I felt that I could not publish without obtaining explicit permission from the various women.

Fortunately, I was able to arrange a return trip to Mornington Island in October 1973. During two weeks on the island, I read the entire record to each woman as obtained from her. Without exception all of them confirmed its validity and gave me their permission to use it as presented. They also agreed that I could add the information acquired during this second visit.

Throughout my first recording I had used pseudonyms. However, Elsie Roughsey voluntarily expressed her wish to have her real name used. She gave several reasons for this, saying, 'I have nothing to be ashamed of and you have written about my life as I have known and lived it. I want the world to know what life is like on Mornington Island. If any student can learn anything from it, I will be pleased.'

During this second visit, I was living in the home of Elsie and Dick. I repeatedly brought up the subject of their blanket permission to publish the material as it was written, pointing out the possibility of its being read by members of their community and by the greater Australian community of which Dick was very much a part. Dick Roughsey had gained prominence both as an Aboriginal artist and a writer. He was a member of several important councils concerned with many aspects of Aboriginal life and activities.

With their understanding of the implications of exposing themselves in this personal way, I felt it only equitable to ask Elsie if she would like to be named as my collaborator. To this she readily agreed. Since my return to the United States she has supplied me with some additional information and I have sent her a copy of the revision, which she approved by writing, 'There is nothing there that I can say you must change because it is all right; nothing wrong about it'.

Research workers studying isolated or preliterate societies in former years paid little attention to the anonymity of their subjects, which at times has undesirable repercussions. Today, 'informed consent' is very much a part of ethical considerations in making clinical observations.

Many anthropologists have commented on this ethical issue. Margaret Mead stated,[20] 'Anthropological research does not have subjects. We work with informants in an atmosphere of trust and mutural respect.' She continued, 'Wanting to know, when what one wants to know is valued by those from whom one must learn it, it is an appeal that few humans can resist . . . the dignity and sensitivity of the informants and their descendants must be considered'.[21] Talcott Parsons stressed the idea of regarding human subjects as participants in a collective, collaborative enterprise.[22] Barnes suggested that 'one way of controlling the effect of publication is to make sure that those affected agree to what is being said about them'.[23] He urged that the informants check the accuracy of the statements and agree to their appearing in print, although their privacy might be invaded and confidences revealed.

I considered my informants to be collaborators. I read them the material, both to ascertain its accuracy and to educate them as to how they might feel if they were to see themselves in print. Most of the information presented was common knowledge among the people of the island, so that few secrets were apt to be revealed.

However, in receiving their consent, I realized that many people would like to have a book written about them. It appeals to one's vanity and other subjective feelings, as well as to the intellectual curiosity that it may enlist. In spite of my efforts to ensure that my informants had full knowledge concerning the implication of giving me permission to publish, no doubt a number of subjective factors of which they were unaware contributed to their willingness. For this reason, I have slightly camouflaged certain aspects of the material where it does not distort the reality of the situation. Several of the women in the original group were no longer on the island in 1973, so that I was not able to obtain their permission. In the reporting of these, certain intimate details were deleted or disguised.

Should this book be read by the Mornington Island people, I trust that they will realize how much I appreciate the cooperation of the various informants and that they will also respect the confidentiality of the content which may not have been general knowledge.

Rapport and Cultural Differences

The relative ease with which the material was collected from most of the informants indicates that trust and rapport were readily established. Although our cultural backgrounds were different, most of these women did not regard me as so foreign to them as to be unable to relate to me. The exceptions were those who refused to grant interviews or who failed to keep appointments. This probably reflected a mixture of resentment, shyness, and anxiety about potential questions. They were unaccustomed to this type of conversation. No doubt other cultural differences also played a part. However, as will be seen, many of the women were pleased to be interviewed and enjoyed the opportunity to talk and express their ideas. Some apparently experienced the interviews as therapeutic.

There is no doubt that the life-histories reveal that I was to a certain extent seeing these Aboriginal women through my middle-class white American eyes and interpreting some of the information according to my own ethnocentric bias. It may be relevant to report some of my subjective responses to living in an Aboriginal community and relating to women who, superficially at least, might be considered to be eons apart from my own cultural background.

Having daily and relatively intimate contact with people whose skin is dark was no novelty to me. The city in which I live and work has a population in which over half of the inhabitants are black. I suspect that I felt much more comfortable among the Aborigines than the majority of urban Australians, who rarely relate to people with skin colour different from their own. Life in the Aboriginal community under study was relatively uncomplicated and lacked the kinds of pressures that are typical of competitive Western cities. It was reminiscent of my childhood spent in a rural American village. I felt that I could identify with the people as being 'country folk'. Of course, these Aboriginal women did not have the creature comforts that I have always known — nor did I have them in their village.

One indication of the cultural distance between us was their apparent lack of curiosity about myself, my life, and my country. I attempted to be open with them and would ask if there were questions they would like to ask me. A few could express slight interest by wondering about such things as how I had come to Australia, by plane or boat, but little more than this. I had identified myself as a physician, not additionally as a psychiatrist. Perhaps my customary attitude of remaining somewhat anonymous in doctor-patient relationships carried over, making it more difficult for the women to question me.

Turning now to the main body of the study, the book essentially is divided into three parts. Chapters two, three and four describe Mornington Island and its people in three different time periods: prior to the advent of white man, at the time of my first visit in 1970, and again in 1973.

Chapters five to nine present the life-history of my collaborator, Elsie Roughsey. Chapters ten to twelve contain vignettes of the lives of the other middle-aged Lardil, the younger Lardil, and finally the Kaiadilt women.

The biographical material is given in a straightforward manner, frequently verbatim. The only editing that occurs was done in the service of clarity or grammar. It might be said that I obtained, and now present, what Malinowski called 'the Native's point of view . . . *his* vision of *his* world'.[24] In this version, it is *her* vision of *her* world. I only occasionally intrude my ideas into the biographical reports.

In the last two chapters I discuss various facets of the women's versions of their lives. In the section entitled 'Reflections', I attempt to consolidate some of the aspects of their life-stories and make some suggestions as to the meaning or function of their attitudes and beliefs. In the final chapter, called 'Psychocultural Adaptation', more theoretical considerations are addressed; I utilize socio-cultural and psychoanalytic hypotheses in discussing current aspects of adaptation of the people of Mornington Island and their potential for change. In my theoretical presentation I attempt to synthesize certain psychoanalytical and anthropological theses pertinent to the subject of adaption in a people undergoing transition in their life style.

The material was not obtained in a classical psychoanalytic situation in which a contract is made with the patient to say whatever comes to mind without censor (free association), in which resistances (defenses) are worked with, in which a transference neurosis is a vital part of the process, and in which interpretations are made. While I do offer certain psychodynamic speculations, I refrain from making interpretations, as I consider this would represent 'wild' analysis, in the sense that they cannot be verified through validation by the person. At times I have stepped out of my role of information gatherer to become the physician-counsellor, offering suggestions to a few individuals, who were asking for help concerning personal matters.

The simplicity of the biographical material and the complexity of efforts at offering theoretical explanations may appear discordant. However, the reader is free to react to the life stories from his own frame of reference.

Notes

1. Sigmund Freud, 'Analysis of a Phobia in a Five Year Old Boy,' 1909. *Standard Edition of Complete Psychological Works,* ed. James Strachey, London, Hogarth Press, 1955, 10:5-148; Sigmund Freud, 'Notes upon a Case of Obsessional Neurosis,' 1909, ibid., pp. 153-221; Sigmund Freud, 'Psychoanalytic Notes on an Autobiographical Account of a Case of Paranoia,' 1911. ibid., 12:9-35.
2. Louis Gottschalk, Clyde Kluckhohn and Robert Angell, *The Use of Personal Documents in History, Anthropology and Sociology.* New York, Social Science Research Council Bulletin 53, 1945, pp. 177-232.
3. ibid., pp. 79-163.
4. Abram Kardiner, *Psychological Frontiers of Society.* New York, Columbia University Press, 1945, p. 448.
5. L. L. Langness, *The Life History in Anthropological Science.* New York, Holt, Rinehart and Winston, 1965, p. 51.
6. Charles C. Hughes, 'Life History in Cross-cultural Psychiatric Research', in *Approaches to Cross-Cultural Psychiatry,* Jane N. Murphy and Alexander H. Leighton, (eds). Ithaca, Cornell University Press, 1966, p. 288.
7. Joyce D. Batty, *Namatjira - Wanderer Between Two Worlds.* Melbourne, Hodder and Stoughton, 1963; Harry Gordon, *The Embarrassing Australian.* Melbourne, Lansdowne Press, 1962; Douglas Lockwood, *I, The Aboriginal. Phillip Roberts* Adelaide, Rigby, 1962; Lionel Rose, *Lionel Rose: Australian: The Life Story of a Champion.* As told to Rod Humphries Sydney, Angus and Robertson, 1969.
8. Jeremy Beckett, 'Man: A Study of Two Half Caste Aborigines', *Oceania* 29, 1958, pp. 91-108; W. E. H. Stanner, 'Durmugam, A Nangiomeri', in *The Company of Man,* ed., Joseph B. Casagrande New York, Harper and Row, 1960, pp. 63-100.
9. Dick Roughsey, *Moon and Rainbow.* Sydney, A. H. and A. W. Reed, 1971.
10. Marie Reay, 'The Social Position of Women', in *Australian Aboriginal Studies,* Australian Institute of Aboriginal Studies Melbourne, Oxford University Press, 1963, pp. 319-333.
11. Catherine Berndt, 'Commentary on the Social Position of Women by Marie Reay', ibid., p. 335.
12. Phyllis Kaberry, *Aboriginal Woman, Sacred and Profane.* London, George Routledge and Sons, 1939.

13. Ronald M. Berndt and Catherine H. Berndt. *Sexual Behaviour in Western Arnhem Land.* New York, Wenner-Gren Foundation for Anthropological Research, Inc., No. 16, 1966).

14. Fay Gale, (ed.) *Woman's Role in Aboriginal Society.* Australian Institute of Aboriginal Studies, Canberra, 1970.

15. Jane Goodale, *Tiwi Wives.* Seattle: University of Washington Press, 1971.

16. John Cawte, *Cruel, Poor and Brutal Nations.* Honolulu, University Press of Hawaii, 1972.

17. William Howells, *The Pacific Islanders.* New York, Charles Scribner's Sons, 1973, p. 155.

18. A. P. Elkin, *The Australian Aborigines.* Garden City, New York, Doubleday & Co., Inc., 1964, p. 12.

19. Roughsey, *Moon and Rainbow.* op. cit.

20. Margaret Mead, 'Research with Human Beings: A Model Derived from Anthropological Field Practice', *Daedalus* 98, 1969, p. 361.

21. ibid, p. 364.

22. Talcott Parsons, 'Research with Human Subjects and the Professional Complex', *Daedalus* 98, 1969, pp. 325-360.

23. John Barnes, 'Some Ethical Problems in Modern Field Work', *British Journal of Sociology* 14, 1963, p. 128.

24. Bronislaw Malinowski, *Argonauts of the Western Pacific.* New York, E. P. Dutton & Co., Inc., 1950, p. 25.

2
The Island and
Its People Before 1915

Mornington Island lies in the subequatorial zone of Australia, in Queensland, in the Gulf of Carpentaria. It is the largest of six islands making up the Wellesley group; in the Ice Age all were undoubtedly a part of the mainland. The Aboriginal people indigenous to Mornington Island are called Lardil.

As far as is known, when the island was discovered in 1802 by Lieutenant Matthew Flinders of the Royal Navy, the Lardil were living there. They had little or no subsequent contact with the European world until the island was again visited in the early part of this century. However, they had exchanges (frequently hostile) with the Aborigines who then lived on the other smaller islands of the Wellesley group. On their primitive rafts, the Lardil also reached the Gulf area of the mainland and made contact with the Aborigines inhabiting that area. Although their dialects differed, they were able to understand each other.

Starting in 1908, the Chief Protector of the Queensland Aborigines compiled annual reports which were included in the Queensland Parliamentary Papers. In 1909, Richard B. Howard, the Chief Protector of the Queensland Aborigines, recorded the following concerning his contact with the indigenous of Mornington Island.

On arrival, I endeavoured to find natives, but although there were plenty of tracks and recent camps, no natives were seen . . . Later, a few natives were seen on the beach . . . three men and three women . . . After many fruitless efforts . . . at last they were induced to come by dinghy to our boat. We offered them food, such as bread, beef, sugar, etc., but although they readily tasted it, they immediately spat it out, evidently not relishing the white man's food, and knew nothing of the use of tobacco. The mirrors aboard seemed to be the greatest attraction and caused considerable amazement.

The next day several of us went ashore again to look over the island . . . Again we encountered no natives until we returned to the beach . . . Some fifty or sixty natives were seen, who at first were most alarmed at our approach . . . We finally obtained sufficient of their confidence to come to close quarters. These people, although emaciated in appearance, are quite free from disease of any sort, and are remarkably strong and agile. I venture to say they are the only surviving tribe of Aborigines in Queensland . . . who have escaped contact with white man. Their food consists principally of fish, nuts, yams and the fruit of pandanus . . . Later, I persuaded them to take me to their main camp . . . I estimate that there are at least 300 natives on Mornington.

The report goes on to say that 'steps should be taken to preserve the occupants on the island from the baneful results that follow the indiscriminate association with whites'. The Chief Protector recommended that a suitable officer should reside on the island and that his duty would be to put a fair area under suitable crops and generally to instruct the natives.[1]

It was in 1914 that the Presbyterian Mission Board established contact with the Lardil by sending missionaries, the Reverend and Mrs Robert Hall, and Mr and Mrs Owen. They made tours of the island offering provisions, friendship, and evangelism. In 1917, the Reverend Robert Hall was murdered by a Lardil who had recently returned to the island after spending many years on the mainland. Some of the other Lardil turned against the three remaining missionaries who were able to defend themselves in the Mission house until help arrived ten days later.

The missionary couple who replaced them were the Reverend and Mrs R. W. Wilson, who remained until 1940 and were very influential in shaping the lives of the present island people.

What were the beliefs, practices, and life styles of the Lardil prior to coming under the administration and teachings of the Mission? There have been no published anthropological studies concerning the Lardil. The best source of information of the traditional customs and beliefs is that recorded in Dick Roughsey's autobiography.[2] Some additional background material was obtained from the book by John Cawte,[3] which dealt with the people of Mornington Island. Gully Peters, a very respected Lardil, now in his seventies, is probably the most reliable living informant who experienced some of the traditional life and practices. He was about fifteen years of age when the first missionary arrived. Others of the indigenous people, as well as the Reverend

Douglas Belcher M.B.E., the missionary in residence from 1945 to 1972, added to the history of 'The Island and Its People'. The following is a compilation.

The Lardil with whom I spoke had learned much about the traditional beliefs mainly by talking with the old folk. As will be seen, when my informants were children, powerful influence was exerted by the missionary and his wife, so that the intermittent contact with their own people did not provide the natural transmission of their customs and myths. Also, the early missionaries soon persuaded the older people to discontinue some of their important tribal practices, especially the initiation ceremony.

When I attempted to obtain historical information, I frequently encountered contradictions, from one informant to another, or by a single informant. For example, when I was trying to clarify, with Dick, something about kinship that he had recorded in his book, he replied in his usual good humour, 'Well, I must have made a mistake.'

The Lardil divided themselves into four local groups according to the winds.

Wind	Area	People
North	Jerrgurum	Jerrgurumbende
South	Larum	Larumbende
East	Lelum	Lelumbende
West	Balum	Balumbende

Each local group consisted of several family camps, containing fifteen to twenty people. Each camp owned a portion of the land, and the water adjacent to it, called littorals. For social and ceremonial grouping, the Lardil divided themselves into halves (moieties), that is, Windward (South and East), and Leeward (North and West).

The camp life was semi-sedentary. They would visit each other as part of celebrations or to obtain foodstuffs not available in their particular area. However, if fish or other food were obtained in an area belonging to another group, it could be taken only with the permission of the owners of the area. Frequently, half of what was collected was extracted as payment by the owners.

The people probably ate well because of the abundant sea life and the natural flora and fauna on the island. It was their custom to feast on whatever was caught or gathered at any one time. Only when this was depleted, would they start their hunting and gathering again. They had developed no way of preserving food. The women gathered berries, nuts, yams, roots, and corms of water lilies, as well as honey from the native 'sugar-bag' bee. They also killed goannas (a kind of lizard), flying foxes, and small birds. The men hunted for wallaby and land birds, but spent most of their efforts spearing or netting fish, dugong (sea cow), and sea turtles. This includes only a small list of the natural food available. While the men and women foraged for food, the old people stayed in the family camp with the small children.

They went naked. Pubic tassels made of human hair or wallaby skin, strung from a fibre belt, were used in ceremonies. During the rainy season, they constructed bush and bark shelters, but otherwise lived and slept in the open.

Their eight subsection system for classification of kinsmen was frequently circumvented when arranging specific marriages. 'Right-head' or 'straight-head' were the terms used for correct marriage partners under their system, in contrast to 'right-skin' which is the kinship term used by most Aborigines. The Lardil system was based on cross-cousin marriage and, according to Dick Roughsey, it was important to know who were considered sisters and brothers and who were cousins. Dick explained the kinship system as follows:

My father's brother is not my uncle; he is also called my father. I call his children brother and sister and they are the same as my own brothers and sisters. My father's sister, however, is called aunt, and I call her children cousins.

My mother's sister is also called my mother, and I call her children brother and sister. My mother's brother is called uncle; he is the one responsible for my initiation and teaching. I call his children cousins. I can marry a cousin from either my mother's or father's side, but usually from my mother's side.

Apart from my father's real brothers, there are also men on the same side of the tribal division as himself whom he would also call brother and whom I would call father — even though they might be only distantly related by blood. I would call the children of these tribal fathers, brother and sister also.

It is the same with my father's sister and my mother's brother. They also have tribal (not actual) brothers and sisters, and I would call their children cousins. It would probably be one of these tribal cousins that I would marry.[4]

When I discussed with Dick the kinship system of the Lardil, as he had written it, he decided that he had 'made a mistake'. One could not marry a cousin from either side as that could have resulted in actual first-cousin marriages, which were prohibited. Their eight subsection kinship system is so complex that it need not concern us here. In tracing the genealogies with the Roughseys and others, it became evident that the Lardil had been quite flexible in following their system and had manipulated it in many ways for their convenience. This was in all probability a necessity in so small a population.

Polygyny (a man had more than one mate at a time) was practiced.

When a father had several wives, all were called mother by the children he fathered (or claimed). The same held if the mother married more than once, all the husbands were known as father. This eliminated the designation of stepfather or stepmother. All children of a father or mother were known as brothers and sisters, again making the designation of 'step' unnecessary. *Gundtha* was the name for both the real and tribal fathers, and *ngama* for the real mother. Older tribal brothers were designated as *thabu* and the younger as *gungu*. Father's sister's sons and mother's brother's sons are cousin-brothers, *yuwardin,* that is, cross-cousins (first cousins).

According to Gully Peters, 'In the old days some of the marriages were right-head and some were wrong. If a husband died, his widow was supposed to belong to his younger brother, but any man might come and take her. Some people would make love to anyone. If a woman had sex with a man other than her husband, the lover might be killed and the wife would be given a good hiding.'

A girl might be 'promised' to a much older man at birth. While waiting for her to grow up he was expected to give gifts to the girl's father. When she reached pubescence (had breast development according to Gully Peters), the girl's parents would fulfil the promise by building a windbreak in the vicinity of the man's camp and taking water and fire to it. Then the mother and her brother, the girl's uncle, would bring the young bride to the area. Next the intended-husband's grandfather and uncle would bring him to the girl. They were told to live together, not to fight, and to stay with each other. This was the marriage ceremony.

If a man had several wives, it is not clear whether they all had been promised or were right-head according to the kinship rules. A young wife might have to wait years until her old husband died before she could have a mate closer to her own age.

Gully also said that boys would be promised to older women and would marry them. The older woman to whom Gully had been promised, died before he was old enough for the marriage to have been consummated. Elsie Roughsey's version of this practice was that a young boy would be promised to an older woman, but that her responsibility was to look after him if something happened to his parents; a role somewhat comparable to that of Godmother or guardian in Western practice.[5]

As we will learn from what the various women have to say, the kinship system still plays a potent role in the lives of the people, despite the fact that being promised at birth is now infrequently practiced. Most of the young people who marry choose each other, but if they choose a wrong-head partner, or even a right-head one, this may have far-reaching repercussions.

Many of the traditional practices and beliefs continue to be an important part of the lives of the people, especially of those who are middle-aged. However, as would be expected from the discontinuity of their exposure to tribal life resulting from the hiatus produced by the advent of the Mission, and from the continuing Western influences, there are many discrepancies and inconsistencies in the present-day recounting and reliving of the traditional customs. The detailed accounts of these beliefs as understood by the contemporary Mornington people will be related by the women themselves.

Totemism has been considered by anthropologists as one of the most important aspects of traditional Aboriginal culture. It implies that there is a common life shared by man and nature.[6] However, my informants seemed to have little awareness of this concept and its traditional importance. There is no word in the Lardil language that means totem. The word *jildreed* (hair) was used for this concept. My informants knew their totems, but most could say little more than that they were handed down from their fathers, much as a surname would be. They had some awareness that totems were related to territorial rights.

One older man had this to say about his totem, 'Mine is the burramundi (a local fish). It was handed down from my father, grandfather, great grandfather. All of their children had this totem. The totems were sacred. They could not be looked at, or killed. You were not allowed to eat your totem. The only exception was if the person was very young and didn't know the difference; he might eat it. He would get sick and vomit. The totem is part of man's life coming from creation. If I go to the mainland and someone asks me what my totem is, I say "burramundi". If he has the same totem, we immediately call each other brother. I have another totem, which is called devil-devil, which means ghost. It is a dreamtime totem. It is a spirit.' However, later this same informant talked of spearing burramundi.

Gully Peters said that he had many totems: the white-faced fish hawk, dugong, and the porpoise, to mention a few. However, he claimed it was not forbidden to kill your totems and eat them, as you could otherwise go very hungry.

In spite of the paucity of information collected from my female informants, Dick Roughsey's book contains many legends indicating that the original Lardil had a rich assortment of myths revealing their belief that man and natural species shared a common life. The rainbow serpent is a common and popular totem among the Lardil, as among many Aboriginal groups. The legend of Thuwathu, the rainbow serpent, as paraphrased from Dick Roughsey is:

Thuwathu came from the south with a mob of people; the stingray, the bluefish, the seagull, white crane, native bee, wallaby, turtle, dugong, and others. Rainbow Serpent built a big humpy (shelter). A big storm arose and his sister, Bulthugu, the rock-cod, implored him to allow her to put her baby daughter into his humpy for protection, but Thuwathu refused. In anger, Bulthugu put a torch to his humpy. Thuwathu, with his flesh burning, started crawling all over the countryside. He vomited as he went, leaving mud crabs, fish, sugar-bag bees, swamp turtle and water lilies. His ribs fell out and these became gidgea trees now used for boomerangs. His blood on the salt pans made red ochre. Finally, he died and a big spring came up. Now the travels of Thuwathu, the Rainbow Serpent, is marked by a river and all the food he left us people.

According to Dick, the moral of this legend, which was danced and sung at an initiation, is that it was the law that a man must look after his sister's children.[7]

It was this uncle, *gagu,* mother's brother, who was the guiding adult in initiating a youth into manhood. Through the circumcision intitiation period, which could last for several years, the initiate learned the secrets of hunting, the use of weapons, and the tribal laws and myths. In this way he was born into spiritual life, that is, the Dreaming.[8]

When the uncle thought that the young man was ready for initiation, he would arrange for the rites. After the ritual dancing that could continue for days, the foreskin for the initiate was cut off, using a stingray barb as a knife. Women would be introduced into the cermony for the purpose of ritual intercourse. The sex secretions were collected in a bark container and drunk by the initiates to insure potency and manliness. Then the initiate would be under the tutelage of his uncle for about six months. He was taught a secret language called *damin* and then was told what girl had been chosen to be his wife. The last phase of the initiation ceremony was called *warama* (subincision) and was not performed until after the man was married. He would ask a brother-in-law who was fully initiated to cut open his penis along the underneath for about half an inch. He was then a fully initiated man.

It was the circumcision rites that so shocked the early missionaries that they soon forbade them. The discontinuance of this practice may be a factor contributing to some of the loss of status of the male Lardil since they felt deprived of the opportunity to become real men.[9]

It was an ancient belief that hardly anyone, except the very old and very young died a natural death: that death was a result of sorcery. Belief in sorcery continues to be present in the minds of many of the present-day Lardil as will be recounted by Elsie and a number of the women. *Lababridi* was the Lardil word for sorcery; however, currently this belief is referred to as *puri-puri*. This latter term, copied from the nearby mainland Aborigines, who are now considered to have the greatest potential to be sorcerers, will be used in this book.

Other traditional beliefs, such as *malgri*, and the magical power of stones to cure illness, remain as viable concepts. 'Pay back', (the act of getting even with someone who has done you wrong), continues to be acceptable to some. However, this does not depend on magic.

In the old days, conception was thought to result from the entrance of a 'baby spirit' into a woman, literally by incorporation. The baby spirit was believed to dwell in certain fish which were caught by the husband and eaten by the wife.

Several of the older people reported that their parents had told them that when a person died his body would go to the east *(maurwa)* and turn into a white person. In his book, Dick Roughsey has a fascinating description of the Lardil religion and burial practices. To quote him, 'We had our own hell and heaven . . . When I die, I still hope to see the Good Country, and it doesn't matter if it is called Heaven or Yili-jilit-nyea.[10]

Notes

1. Richard B. Howard, Queensland Aboriginals, Chief Protector, Report in *Queensland Parliamentary Papers*, 1909, Vol. 2, pp. 970-973.
2. Dick Roughsey, *Moon and Rainbow*. Sydney, A. H. & A. W. Reed, 1971.
3. John Cawte, *Cruel, Poor and Brutal Nations*. Honolulu, University Press of Hawaii, 1972.
4. Roughsey, op. cit., p. 26.
5. The custom of a boy marrying an older woman is reminiscent of the practices of the Tiwi group of Aborigines. Among the Tiwi there were no unmarried women. However, I was not able to obtain any information to support a comparable practice among the Lardil. See C. W. M. Hart and Arnold R. Pilling, *The Tiwi of North Australia*. New York, Holt, Rinehart and Winston, 1960, pp. 14-21.
6. For an excellent discussion of the complex subject of totemism see: A. P. Elkin, *The Australian Aborigines*. Garden City, N. Y., Doubleday & Co., Inc., 1964, pp. 139-164.
7. Roughsey, op. cit., pp. 23-26.
8. Dreaming: A term used in the literature for the Aboriginal socio-religious complex of ideas about the universe, the creative epoch, the after-life in the relation of man to other species and natural objects. Actually, the present Lardil use the term Dreamtime (and occasionally Dreamland) when referring to the socio-religious ideas.
9. Virginia Huffer, 'Australian Aborigine: Transition in Family Grouping', *Family Process* 12, 1973, p. 310.
10. Roughsey, op. cit. p. 93.

3
The Island and Its People in 1970

The influence of the Presbyterian Mission in over fifty years of supervision brought profound changes in the life of the Mornington Island Aborigines. For over twenty years the Reverend and Mrs R. Wilson were in residence. It was they who, in the early 1920s, established a 'dormitory system'[1] to provide a kind of boarding school for the children of the Aborigines.

In addition to the indigenous Lardil offspring, Aboriginal children from the neighbouring Gulf country of mainland Australia were sent to the Mornington Island dormitory. These children, usually waifs, represented several coastal tribes; a few were of mixed racial descent, part Chinese or part European. Most were quite young when they arrived at Mornington. Having spent their developing and adult years on the island, they have been absorbed for the most part into the Lardil group.

In the dormitory system, girls and boys lived in separate buildings. The children were given English names by the Missionary, who taught them to speak the English language. They were instructed in reading, writing and arithmetic, and in the Christian religion.

The influence of the Mission extended into most aspects of the community. Over the years, the adults gradually deserted their family littorals and moved to an area immediately adjacent to the Mission, forming what has come to be referred to as 'the village'. The remainder of the island has been left to the animals and the fairly dense vegetation.

Thus, life has become settled for these people. Many of the traditional practices have been eliminated and the Western model of monogamous marriage has become the accepted practice. The Lardil are no longer the 'emaciated', shy natives described in the Chief

Protector's report of 1909.

Except for those of mixed racial descent, the Lardil have very dark skin, and slightly curly hair. Their eyes are deep-set with heavy eyebrows. Their noses are deeply indented at the base and flare widely at the nostrils. The women are of medium height, by Western standards, and at present tend to be slightly obese. The men are taller, but more slender. Many have full beards. The thinness of their legs is notable.

In 1948, at their request, the forty-two surviving members of a tribe known as Kaiadilt were brought from their own island, Bentinck, to live on Mornington Island. Tindale had estimated there were one hundred and twenty-three Kaiadilt alive in 1942 and fifty-eight in 1947.[2] Their numbers decimated, they were found in great distress on Bentinck by the Missionary and several Lardil. The Kaiadilt had had minimal contact with any other people and their society was in decay. They have been described by Cawte as 'the earth's most excluded and isolated people'.[3]

The Kaiadilt and their progeny are strikingly different in appearance from the other Aborigines on Mornington Island. While their skin is deep chocolate in colour, they tend to be taller, more slender, and as children have reddish-blonde hair. As they mature only the ends of their hair show this colouration. As they become middle-aged their hair colour changes to tawny or dark brown. It is less curly than that of the Lardil.

As of October of 1970 the population of Aborigines on Mornington Island was six hundred and twenty-seven. Of these, ninety-eight were Kaidilt and the remaining five hundred and twenty-nine were considered to be primarily members of the Lardil group.[4] Over half (336) were under twenty years of age, and of these thirty-five were 'half-castes'.[5] In addition to the Aborigines, there were in 1970, eighteen white inhabitants of the island comprising the Mission staff and their children.

The majority of the Lardil people over thirty years of age had received their education and training in the controlled atmosphere of the dormitory system, which will be described in some detail in a subsequent chapter. As a result of this education, they spoke fluent, though limited, English, and had been imbued with the mores and morals of the white Christian ethic. The younger Lardil lived with their parents, who were from the dormitory background. They attended the Mission school from ages five to sixteen. The younger Lardil used English almost exclusively and did not teach their children the Lardil language.

The Kaiadilt over thirty years of age had experienced no consistent exposure to a culture or tribe other than their own until their evacuation from Bentinck Island. Consequently, the middle-aged ones had minimal ability to use English. Although the Lardil and Kaiadilt languages were similar enough to permit some mutual comprehension, the Kaiadilt language, by comparison had a tonal quality that can only be described as sounding very angry. The younger Kaiadilt, who had attended the Mission school, spoke satisfactory English. They tended to use their native tongue among themselves more than did the Lardil.

Mornington Island is about 65 kilometres long and 13 to 16 kilometres wide. It has two distinct seasons: the dry, from March to November, when the trade wind blows constantly from the south-east; and the wet, from December to March, when 1150 to 1300 millimetres of rainfall is brought by the monsoonal shift of the wind to the north-west. There is a moderately dense growth of savannah woodland covering most areas. Mangrove clumps occur along the coastline.

Because of the long, dry season, and the lack of sufficient water storage for cultivation of any crop, the land has provided little for the increasing population, let alone a surplus for trade. The sea has the protential to provide more, but because of its low depth can be approached only by shallow draft boats at high tide, which occurs only once a day. Furthermore, the export of local seafood such as barramundi, sea turtle, and rock oysters would require a system of refrigeration in order to be feasible.

While there are 965 square kilometres that make up the island of Mornington, in 1970 all of the inhabitants lived in the village at its western tip, adjacent to the Mission. This type of settled village life is aberrant from the traditional camp life of fifteen to twenty people. It allows for no privacy, so gossip is pervasive. Interpersonal difficulties arising from this will be dealt with later.

Most of the dwellings were constructed of corrugated iron or aluminum sheeting. A few built of wood were painted a pleasing light pink shade. Although the majority were of galvanized iron, there was much variation in construction. Those houses built to provide greater comfort stood off the ground on concrete pilings 1 to 2 metres in height, to allow for coolness and dryness. Some appeared to have been prefabricated, with window frames, sashes, and a peaked roof. In others, the windows were just openings cut out of the iron and hinged for moveability. The so-called 'dirt floor' houses were built directly on the ground, with no flooring, and with a flat roof. The houses usually had only one room, or at most, two. The furnishings inside consisted mainly of cots or mats for sleeping which were easily moved outside when the weather would be too hot for sleeping inside. The bedclothes were usually rumpled because the cots served as chairs. There were numerous boxes or cheap suitcases used to store clothing and any other possessions. Several shelves held crockery and miscellaneous utensils. There might have been an occasional chair or table. Inside some of the houses everything was neatly arranged, in others, disarray was extreme.

There was electricity in the houses, but only for light. A few householders proudly owned kerosene refrigerators. Although several houses had wood-burning stoves, most of the cooking was done outside on open fires, so that the need for utensils other than billycans and frying pans hardly existed. All had outside toilets. These had sealed pans that were emptied twice weekly by the sanitation crew, and were remarkably free of flies and odor.

A few yards surrounding the houses were enclosed by fences, topped by ever-present barbed wire. The barbed wire was used as clotheslines with the barbs serving as clothespins. It was reported to be unusual for anyone to cut themselves on this type of wire. Although the yards were bare of grass during the long, dry season, the ground was usually swept. When the poinciana trees and oleanders were in bloom and the mangoes were ripening, there were some beautiful vistas, with the pale-blue sea in the background and neighbouring Denham Island in the distance. There were several varieties of creeping vines with purple or yellow flowers. For the most part, however, in the village area there was nothing but loose sand and more loose sand. As soon as the rains came, the sand became packed down and, in a miraculous fashion, grass appeared.

Most of the Lardil lived on each side of a gully which was green even at the end of the dry season, because of the type of couch (Bermuda) grass that grew there. Beyond was a higher ridge where the homes tended to be of better quality. Here, twenty new dwellings were being constructed in 1970. In one area of the village there was a slight ridge near the water, and it was there that the Kaiadilt lived in their own minute enclave. The construction here was the poorest.

In the village a few chickens wandered around. There were hardly any dogs, which was uncharacteristic of other Aboriginal settlements.[6] However, children were everywhere. All were without clothing until they were about five or six, the age when they entered school. The children invited attention, delighted in being greeted, and loved to laugh and tease. This was especially true of the young Kaiadilt. This type of interaction seemed to be a part of the *joie de vivre* of childhood, because they certainly did not lack attention from the adult. Most of the women, no matter what they were doing, had several children in their arms or clambering over them. It was not unusual to see that same type of bodily contact between fathers and their children. Indeed, the older children picked up the younger ones and played around with them as the women did.

The Aboriginal women wore cotton dresses that looked well laundered. Comb and brush were seldom used. Most went barefooted. Occasionally, sandals or scuffs were worn. The exception occurred among the older Kaiadilt women, whose dresses tended to be in tatters, exposing much of their bodies. A few of the younger Lardil women dressed and groomed themselves in such a manner that they were considered 'smart dressers' by the islanders.

The main daily activities for the women consisted of carrying water from the wells, washing clothes in large metal drums that were often very rusty and waiting around the Mission store for their meagre orders to be filled. Of course, there was sweeping, cooking, and minding the children; but there was also much time for yarning, or just doing nothing. Some of women supplemented their family's diet by fishing from the shore with hand lines. In this settled village life, collecting native foods by the women had almost ceased except during bush holidays.

Probably about thirty to thirty-five women were dedicated to the Church and the choir, the Ladies Group and whatever other activity the

Lardil women at the village well in 1970

Mission was sponsoring. However, religious fervour was not evident. There was a small library under the direction of one of the school teachers, and a few were regular patrons of it.

There was very little opportunity for paid employment for the women. A few had cooking and cleaning duties at the small hospital, several were teacher's assistants or worked in the Mission office, and some were domestics for the Mission staff. The wages were very low, as were all the Mission wages. A number of the women assisted their husbands in handcrafts, but that was primarily a male occupation.

The men of the island dressed in cotton trousers and frequently wore white shirts. A few had adopted the shorts, turtle neck sweaters, and knee-length socks popular with white Australians. Employment for men was not quite as limited as for women. In 1970, there were two projects that provided jobs for those most willing to work. One project at Birri, an area about 30 kilometres from the village, was the digging of wells to provide water for cattle-raising and the cultivation of fruit and vegetables.

The second opportunity for male employment was the construction of the twenty new houses for which the Queensland Government furnished supplies. Traditional handcraft skills were retained by a number of the men. Their craftgoods, which include boomerangs, spears, shields, and drone pipes, were sold through the Mission, and had a good market. In addition, some were employed at the Mission, itself, in various capacities, including unloading the supply boat, emptying the latrines, and maintaining the airstrip.

Some of the men, in order to provide food for their own families and others, as well as for sport, went hunting with spears for fish, sea turtle, and dugong, However, guns were used to shoot an occasional wallaby or water bird. The popularity of water activities could be appreciated by the number of dinghies that had been purchased individually or by groups in the community. In 1970, there were about twelve such craft, usually made of fibreglass, with high-powered outboard motors. There was little other sports activity. Cricket teams had just been organized. After five in the afternoon, on the shady side of the many houses, the men often gathered to play cards, with or without gambling. Music from transistor radios could be heard.

The monotony of life on this remote island was broken twice a week by the arrival of the scheduled plane from Mt Isa, 500 kilometres to the south, bringing expected or unexpected guests or residents, as well as mail and perishable supplies. Each time at least 100 people gathered to greet the plane, and the amount of activity at the airstrip was surprising to the newcomer. In addition, several charter planes frequently landed each week, usually with white people who came for a variety of reasons, such as for government or Mission affairs, for sport fishing, or for personal interests.

Although getting off the island required money for air fares, a surprising number of Aborigines came and went. It was somewhat difficult for the Mornington people to find employment off the island. Previously, both men and women worked on stations (cattle and sheep ranches), but this opportunity lessened with the recent passage of minimum wage laws. While Aborigines worked well as domestics or stockmen, the life on stations was one of lonely isolation from their own families and countrymen. The problems encountered by Aborigines working in Australian towns were all too well known, including discrimination by Europeans and the difficulty created by alcohol. As a result, only a few island people were working elsewhere. With the help of Mission or government funds, several of those children considered by their teachers to be promising students went to the mainland for a more advanced education or specialized training. Many return home, however, without having completed their studies.

The health of the islanders appeared, at least superficially, to be good, except for obvious chronic respiratory infections. Hookworm infestation, which used to be frequent, had been almost eradicated by a programme of the Queensland Health Department. Anaemia was at one time common among young children; now they were given a daily supplementary feeding of protein and vitamins at the hospital. However, considering the inadequacy of the diet of many of the adults, one would wonder what a nutritional survey would reveal. The staple diet consisted of tea, and damper (a bread-like cake consisting of flour, water, baking soda, and fat drippings) cooked in a skillet over an open fire. With some regularity this was supplemented by tinned or fresh meat and canned fruit, rice, potatoes, and onions, all purchased at a store in the Mission area. In addition to the protein from the seafoods, bullocks (steers) were killed twice weekly and sold at 40 cents a pound. Apples and oranges were brought by aeroplane, when it was not loaded with passengers, luggage or other items.

A fifteen-bed hospital and clinic were under the supervision of the Flying Doctor Service of Queensland. However, the great majority of the medical, surgical, and obstetrical work was carried out in a responsible and exemplary fashion by two nursing sisters. The school, which the children attended from the ages of five to sixteen, was then staffed by four white teachers and three local assistants. In addition, several white male Mission staff members supervised the general maintenance work and the new projects.

The Mission, for the past eighteen years, was under the direction of a most understanding couple, the Reverend and Mrs Douglas Belcher.

They had appreciated the creativity of the people and had taken an interest in their tribal legends, crafts, and some of their customs. The Reverend Douglas Belcher interpreted the Bible, especially the Old Testament, in terms that the people could apply to their own everyday life and their customary laws and traditions. He had encouraged the continuation of their handcraft ability as well as their native dance, the corroboree. In addition to being the Minister, he had general administrative duties and was an advisor in their difficulties and disputes.

There was an attempt at self-government in the village, in that there was a group of Councillors, elected by secret ballot. Women were eligible not only to vote, but to become members of the Council. One woman was, in fact, elected as a Justice of the Peace, but for personal reasons, she had chosen not to serve. The duties and power of the Council were evolving. They could take limited disciplinary action in disputes or infringements against the law among the villagers, but found it difficult to execute this. The Council was involved in certain administrative aspects concerning land use, so that the Aborigines had the authority for leasing part of their area to a company planning to develop a prawn freezing business. With the assistance of the Mission and Queensland Government, the Council shared some of the responsibility for the development of the cattle and garden programmes at Birri.

The standard of living, judged by housing, diet, education and recreation, was lower than in most rural white communities of comparable size in Australia. However, in comparison to many other Aboriginal settlements, this community would be considered superior.

Notes

1. Many Missions of various denominations in Australia developed comparable 'dormitory systems' of education after World War I.
2. Norman Tindale, 'Some Population Changes Among the Kaiadilt People of Bentinck Island, Queensland', *Records of the South Australian Museum* 14, 1962, pp. 299-300.
3. John Cawte, *Cruel, Poor and Brutal Nations.* Honolulu, University Press of Hawaii, 1972, p. 131.
4. There were twelve adults who were of part European or Chinese descent. Three Aborigines had recently moved from the mainland through marriage. These were all identified with the Lardil tribe.
5. Half-caste is the term the people of the island used to refer to those who have one parent of a race other than Aboriginal. In the literature, the terms part-Aboriginal or mixed-blood are usually preferred.
6. All dogs on Mornington Island had been ordered to be killed by a previous missionary, supposedly for health reasons. Now only male dogs, flown in from the mainland, are permitted. The expense involved limited the number of families who had a dog.

4
The Island and Its People in 1973

In the three years since my first visit a number of changes had taken place. First, three planes a week came in from Mt Isa, instead of two. When I arrived it was good to see so many familiar faces among the Aborigines and to feel warmly greeted by them. However, I recognized none of the Mission staff as there had been a complete change in personnel.[1] Even the Reverend and Mrs Douglas Belcher had been transferred to another reserve.

The excitement at the airstrip upon my return was probably not so much to greet me, as to see one of the Lardil dancing groups, consisting of seven men, departing for Sydney. They were to perform their native dance, the corroboree, at the official opening of the Opera House when Queen Elizabeth was to be present. It was evident that the Islanders were thrilled by the fact that their group was to dance for the Queen. Later I learned that five others were to leave in several days to attend the performance.

In addition, two other male corroboree groups were in Melbourne dancing for various affairs. Recently, several other individuals had spent time in Canberra or Melbourne attending meetings concerning Aboriginal affairs or teachers workshops. Obviously, some of the people were having relatively extensive contact with urban Australia.

Among those present to greet me was Elsie Roughsey, my main informant during my previous visit. We immediately embraced and she told me I was her friend, and that I was going to be her guest in her home. Included in the invitation was Dr Nancy Waxler, a sociologist from the Harvard Medical School, who was accompanying me during the first week of my stay. The Roughsey family was now living in one of the new houses, and being invited to stay with them contrasted to the fact that I had not been asked inside their former dwelling during my previous visit. But more about this later.

The twenty new houses that had been started three years previously were all but completed: eighteen were occupied. They were located on a high ridge, parallel to the airstrip, on each side of a new gravel road. They were quite attractive in appearance. All were built 2.5 metres off the ground, resting on metal pilings. The houses were constructed of timber frames, covered by metal sheeting in a number of different and pleasing colours, including green, pink, and yellow. Dick and Elsie Roughsey's house was blue.

The interior walls were of masonite; painted in pastel shades. The doors and floors were of plywood. The windows were of the louvre type, allowing air and dust to blow in. The flooring was also painted, but most of the paint had been absorbed by the plywood. There were three bedrooms, a large area which the architect probably had thought of as a living-dining room, a kitchen, and a bathroom containing a shower and lavatory only. The kitchen contained a sink, a wood stove, and many enclosed cabinets with countertops for working space, as well as hanging cupboards. In addition, most of the occupants had purchased primus stoves. Some of those in which electricity had been installed had refrigerators. When I arrived, electricity had not been extended, as yet, to all the houses. The Roughsey's home, for example, had none. They had no 'fridge' and no light except that provided by torches (flashlights) or kerosene latterns.

Each house had two outside stairways, one up to the front verandah, which extended the entire length of the front of the house; the other led from the kitchen to the backyard where the latrine was located.

The large area under the house contained a double laundry tub with running water. Clotheslines, stretched between the pilings, held the laundry, which dried quickly in the constant warm breeze. Many of the people used this open basement area as a shady place to sit or to work on handcrafts.

The houses were surrounded by large yards. During the dry season no grass grew; however, there were many flowering vines. Old rusty oil drums served as trash receptacles. Frequently, trash did not reach the receptacle. Scattered ashpiles indicated that the people often cooked outside over open fires, rather than use their stoves indoors. Behind each house stood an iron cylinder, constructed so that a fire could be made in the bottom to heat water for boiling clothes. However, since the tap water was tepid, it was not necessarily heated for laundry or bathing. The ample supply of water had been made possible by the completion of a pipeline from a large spring 6.5 kilometres from the village.

The new houses were allocated to applicants on the basis of length of service to the Mission. There was apparently little dissension among the people as to which families were to be allowed to move into the new houses. Perhaps the fact that there was a monthly rent ranging from $6.00 to $12.00, in contrast to no rent for the original dwellings, may have been a factor.

Only one of the Bentinck Island families lived in a new house. For the most part the houses were occupied mainly by the middle-aged couples who, as children, were the dormitory inhabitants. However, in addition to these couples and their unmarried children, many of their married children, grandchildren or other relatives lived with them. It was, therefore, not surprising that the older village area, at least that part that had been inhabited by the Lardil, seemed empty and deserted. Most of the women no longer had to go to the village well for water.

The Kaiadilt camp remained essentially unchanged. The housing was the same as in 1970. Perhaps there were fewer people, as some had chosen to camp on neighbouring Denham Island, and 'commute' by boat to the Mission area for school, supplies or work. About six Kaiadilt had returned to their native island of Bentinck a month before my arrival, where they hoped to set a up a permanent camp.

The Mission area had changed little in three years. Concrete pilings to support a new hospital and additional school rooms were in evidence. However, further construction had been halted as there was disagreement between the local community and the Queensland government, which was financing the buildings, as to the best locations for these two structures. The contractors had just left the island when I got there. They would not return until the differences were resolved.

The store where all supplies were purchased had been reorganized into a self-service type with check-out counters. Previously, the people had had to write out their orders and to wait until they were filled. It was my impression that a greater variety of food-stuffs was available, although there was still a paucity of fresh fruit and vegetables. Butchering of bullocks continued as in 1970.

The school staff had been increased from four to seven teachers, all white, who were paid by the State; the salaries, therefore, were larger than those previously paid by the Mission. The curriculum was being gradually upgraded to comply with that taught throughout Queensland. The Mornington teachers will receive all the equipment supplied to other schools of comparable size throughout the State.

With the vast improvement of the water supply, hoses were being used to water grass and flowers around the school. Some of the people had planted small vegetable gardens and flower beds, as water was now available even at the end of the dry season.

Since there was no longer a minister in residence, one flew up from Mt Isa once a month to conduct services and to spend four days visiting with the people and conducting meetings for them and the Mission staff. When he was not present, the Aborigines and Mission staff conducted the church service.

Another change since 1970 was that beer was now legally allowed on the island. The supply boat was supposed to bring in 300 cases (24 cans to a case) each month. A canteen, open nightly, was permitted to sell a limit of three cans to a man and two cans to a woman. However, the beer supply (only 100 cases had come in on the last boat) had been exhausted a week prior to my arrival. Apparently on that Saturday, some of the men had supplemented the beer with illegal whiskey and a tremendous fight with boomerangs and *nulla nullas* (a rounded or carved piece of wood with a knob at one end) had developed. The resulting injuries filled the hospital beds and kept the two nursing sisters busy suturing for almost twenty-four hours. More about the effect of this 'bash' on the people will be discussed in a later chapter.

So far, most of the changes that I have described were obvious to the eye. However, a much more profound change was in the process of development. The aboriginal community was about to become incorporated and control by the Mission would no longer operate.

According to the Manager, Mr A. M. Gibson, it had always been the Presbyterian Mission Board's policy to eventually work itself out of a job. The philosophy of the Board is that the church has a mission to help people to run their own affairs in a Christian context; not to perpetuate a Mission for its own sake.

The incorporation of the village had been discussed with the Mornington Islanders since 1970. There were no militant Aborigines on the island and no vote of the people had been taken. The withdrawal of the Mission would made incorporation necessary in order to receive money directly from the Government. At the time of my visit in 1973, the papers of incorporation had been drawn up ready for signing, and a Board of Directors had been appointed. Full control was to be assumed on I July, 1974. The name of the island was to the changed to *Gunana*, meaning good camping or hunting ground. The people were to be known as *Gunanamonda*, that is, people of *Gunana*.

The teachers and nursing sisters were to continue to be paid directly by the Queensland Government, but all other affairs were to be decided by the *Gunanamonda*. They were to be free to employ white advisers such as village administrator, store supervisor and others, but the decision to do so was to be theirs. In 1973, in addition to those named previously, the head stockman and other supervisory personnel were all white.

The duties and responsibilities of the corporation were to be many. It would own the new houses, collect rent, and be responsible for repairs. It would control the payroll as well as the dispersement of the various allotments available to them (as well as all Australians).[2] The food and clothing stores would be under its jurisdiction. The handcraft shop operation had been turned over to the people in January 1973. There was some information that indicated that this previously profitable operation was already in debt.

Among other plans in the offing was one to send two Aborigines to Aurukun to a training course to become native ministers.[3] They would be encouraged to develop marriage, burial, baptismal, and other religious ceremonies that would incorporate some of the traditional Aboriginal practices and beliefs. For example, during the baptism ceremony, if a child were immersed into the sea this would symbolically mean that he would become a good fisherman.

The response of the women to the plan for the Aborigines to assume autonomous control of the island is reflected in the comments to be reported in subsequent chapters. The proposed incorporation and the shift of control reflects the hope of the Mission Board. The Mornington Island women will be important figures in the future transition of island life.

Notes

1. Mr A. M. Gibson had been head schoolmaster in 1970, but was on extended leave at that time. In 1973, he was the Mission Manager.
2. Allotments in Australia were available for pensioners, widows, sick, child endowment, unemployment, as well as supporting mothers benefit and secondary school grants to Aboriginal children. This last was the only subsidy for Aborigines only.
3. Aurukan is another Presbyterian Mission, located on the Cape York Peninsula which was also in the process of incorporation.

5
Labbarnor:
Sweetness of the Fig

Elsie Roughsey, who was to become my collaborator, was from our first meeting outside her house quite verbal, open, and comfortable in talking with me. She almost immediately told me that her Lardil name was Labbarnor, which translated means 'sweetness of the fig'. This translation seems appropriate to me. The sweetness of this fruit is not apparent with the first mouthful. Elsie's sweetness became apparent as our friendship grew.

She was of average height (about 163 centimetres), a stocky, dark-skinned woman. Her hair was slightly curly, usually not brushed or combed. Her dresses were clean but tended to be old ones that initially had been used for 'dress-up' occasions such as church, and now showed many years of wear. She almost always was bare-footed. Elsie thought that she was about forty-three to forty-five years of age. She explained that since her parents did not know the calendar years, their births tended to be set by such things as the weather, the season or what fruits were ripe. Elsie Roughsey's life-history will be presented in the various roles in which she has functioned. In this chapter, Labbarnor's early life experiences will be related as she remembered them.

Parents
Elsie was born into a traditional Lardil family; European Christian customs had been introduced to the Islanders less than ten years prior to her birth. Her father, William, practiced polygyny, having two wives, who were biological sisters. To quote Elsie, 'Both were married to him as he was a good fighter and hunter. He could cut a hundred boomerangs, all for war, not craft.[1] My mother couldn't speak English, so she stayed at the camp[2] and went bush hunting for water lilies,

pandanus nuts, roots, goannas, flying foxes, oysters, and other food. She made nets out of bush fibres in which to carry things.

She would come to the Mission and bring fish, crabs, and roots to trade for sugar, flour, and other supplies. We didn't use money, but exchanged food for supplies. I don't remember much about my mother until we were sent to the bush from the Mission during the war years.' Her mother, Lizzie, bore three children: Julie, an older sister; Elsie; and a younger brother, Colin. All currently are respected members of the island community.

Her father's other wife, 'Aunt Maggie', bore him two children: a daughter who moved to a distant city and later died, and a son who died about twenty years ago. Aunt Maggie died when Elsie was about six years old. As Elsie remembers. Aunt Maggie liked her as well as her own two children. 'My father spoke English, but not too well. He worked around the Mission and ran the Mission lugger.[3] I can't tell you much about my parents during my growing years, as I lived in the dormitory.'

Elsie continued, 'I do know where I was "signed" to my parents. It was on that point of land jutting out just about where we went for rock oysters (on the leeward side). If a wife is going to have a baby, but no-one knows it except her, her husband will start having a lot of success in hunting turtles and dugong. Old folks say, he comes with a lot of "tucker".[4] They say *margada* — they are going to have a baby. According to tradition, the unborn baby is "signed" there, and when the baby grows up he will have a part of that country. So by our tribal customs that part belongs to me, as I was "signed" there.'

The Dormitory

'When I was about five or six I'd go to the Mission every morning and just play around. I'd have three meals there and go back to the camp at night. I started living in the dormitory when I was about eight. I think there were about twenty-five girls in all. Some who were brought over from the mainland were very young, say three or four. They never saw their parents again and they would cry and cry.

'We all would live there until we were married (except during the war evacuation period, 1942-1944). We would be locked in from seven o'clock at night to seven in the morning. We learned to read and write English, also obedience and to work. And, of course, about Christianity.

'We were well fed, as in those days the Mission had a garden and cows, goats, and cattle. We'd have porridge with fresh milk. At noon we'd have a big meal of rice with meat and things from the garden: pumpkin, cabbage, carrots, beets, beans, shallots, tomatoes, pineapples, custard apples, lemons, papaws. The children would carry water. The garden disappeared about twenty years ago when the dormitory was closed.[5] For tea we'd have damper, jam, cow's milk. When we had too much food, we'd share it with the people outside. There would be a big feast on Christmas Day.

'There were unhappy times in the dormitory: if girls would fight with me, I'd fight back. I had my older sister on my side. I'd be unhappy if we quarrelled. Some girls loved to tease; they'd make disrespectful comments about my parents, like "Oh, you are a Williams"[6] in a nasty way. I'd get mad, because we were taught to respect our mother and father and not say anything against them. Now I can't imagine why those remarks bothered me so.[7] Now I am pleased to have been Miss Williams and proud to be Mrs Roughsey.

'If we did anything wrong like talk or take something that belonged to someone else, we'd really be punished. Like we'd have to stand in front of the group, be hit on the fingers with rulers or write something a hundred times. If someone did something very bad, she'd have to lie on the scales and be hit on the backside until there were red marks. Sometimes we'd have to go without a meal. I didn't get punished very often.

'But the Missionary and his wife were a good father and mother to us. The Mission lady taught us what to do when we got our periods. She called it "unwell". She or one of the older girls would show us how to keep clean and change cloths. Each of us had four and we learned how to wash them out and hang them to dry. We were told the bleeding was something that would happen each month, and no connection was made with becoming a woman or having babies. The Missionary frightened girls about men, told us to run away from boys. We never wondered how babies got made, like it was a surprise.'[8]

There was a comparable dormitory system for boys, who were permitted only slightly more freedom. The girls were allowed to go on supervised walks, or bathing on Saturday. When they were in their late teens or early twenties, on Sunday afternoons, young men were allowed to visit on the Mission house verandah. Sometimes they would bring the girl who interested them some small gift such as wild honey, a pen, or beads, or perhaps some sweet that they had obtained from the supply boat. This type of courtship was usually awkward, and marked by little communication, verbal or nonverbal.

Marriage was arranged and agreed on in several ways. The young man might express to the Missionary his desire to marry a certain young woman. Then the Missionary, if this seemed suitable to him, and to the girl's parents (if they were alive), would tell the girl. The girl apparently had the privilege of refusing, but rarely did.

While right-head or straight-head marriages were part of the Lardil tradition, there were probably not more than eight dormitory girls who married men according to their traditional kinship rule. What apparently happened more commonly was that the Missionary decided when his charges were of marriageable age, and that a couple had some qualities that might make them compatible mates. He then arranged the union of the young man and woman. According to Elsie, the Missionary 'made them love and trust each other and gave them time to see if they would be true to each other'. How he set about to accomplish this was not clear.

The dormitory was temporarily closed during 1942-1944, when the northern coast of Australia was in imminent danger of invasion by the Japanese. Troops were stationed on the western tip of the island, relatively close to the Mission. The children from the mainland were sent back unless they chose to stay with Lardil families. The local families and their children were encouraged to 'go bush', that is disperse themselves throughout the island. When the threat of invasion passed, most of the girls, including Elsie, returned to the dormitory, as they preferred it to bush living. However, the Mission Board philosophy changed after World War II and the dormitory system was finally abandoned in the early fifties.

Most of the women who had spent all or part of their growing years in this closely controlled and regulated system had positive feelings about it. To quote them, 'The Mission gave us protection, as it was hard to live out in the rain and cold in the "bush" fashion. It gave us an education, and we learned how to work. It taught sports and all kind of games. It taught us to grow up in a Christian way, and not to question things.' The women who lived under this authoritarian system during their developing years realized that the young people of today would not tolerate such an institution. However, in a wishful manner, they thought it would have been good, in that their children would have learned obedience, industriousness, and kindness. None of them directly verbalized that such teaching might be a responsibility of theirs as parents.

Elsie's Parents — Additional Material, 1973

When I returned to the island and read the part concerning her parents to Elsie, she added more information which considerably changed the picture and may account, at least in part, for some of her own attitudes toward sex. In relating this material she seemed more perplexed than is usual for her.

'I've often wondered who would tell me to go to the Mission before I started living there. Somehow I knew that my mother was not living with my father even before I went to dormitory. I was with my father's people. It seems like three old women looked after me. I got so used to the Mission, I had to learn family relationships later. I had only a vague idea who my mother and father were.'

When the dormitory was temporarily closed during the war, Elsie stayed mainly with her father and 'Old Kate' in the village area. Even the details about this period were sparse.

Elsie thought her father left her mother when her younger brother was a year old, and that the boy was cared for by his maternal grandparents (Old Billie and Judy), and his uncle, Jacko. Elsie went on to say, 'My father sneaked with other women all the time. He tried to get back with my mother, but her relatives wouldn't allow it. They fought him and drove him away many times. He lived with different women; the last one was "Old Kate". I stayed with them during the war and called her Mother. She is one of those old people I showed you.[9]

'During the war, sometimes my father would let me go with my mother and her parents. She taught me where to find bush food and swamp turtle. They make nice smooth tracks on the ground. She even taught me to use a cooking stick to spark fire. We would eat as we hunted. She showed me how to paint myself for a corroboree and for a wedding, but I still didn't learn anything about sex.'[10]

Later, when she talked about her mother who died after Elsie's second son was born, I got little feeling of any special mother-daughter relationship. 'I would visit my mother when Dick was away working. She lived on the south side (Larum). She'd be happy to see me, but would get angry if I messed around with any of her things, trying to help her. She called me Labbarnor. She'd talk in Lardil; I'd answer her in English; but we could understand each other. I'd say, "Mum, why not talk English", and try to teach her small words; she'd burst out laughing because she couldn't say them.'

The way Elsie spoke of her father gave the impression that he was more of a 'real' person to her. He died about eight years ago.

It is doubtful that Elsie really 'didn't learn anything about sex'. It is tempting to speculate that because of her suppressed sexual fantasies, perhaps heightened by the Mission admonitions about the opposite sex, Elsie not only made a hero out of her father, but could permit herself to remember the sexual exploits of her father. She remembered her mother as the deserted, asexual woman.

Notes

1. Almost without exception, the women, both Lardil and Kaiadilt, referred to their fathers as 'good fighters and hunters'; obviously not only admirable but necessary

traits for survival. But could all of the men have excelled in these attributes? According to Mr Belcher, it is doubtful if Elsie's father cut any boomerangs prior to the coming of the Mission, which brought steel axes. On this island, traditional weapons were wooden spears and staves. Their cutting instrument was a piece of 'bailer' shell with a serrated edge, made by biting with the teeth. No local rock was suitable for tool making. However, it is possible that the Lardil may have obtained hard stone for axes in trade with mainland Aborigines.

2. Elsie's family 'camp' was on a ridge, within about 200 metres of where Elsie lived in 1970.

3. Lugger: a small ketch rigged boat used in tropical Australian waters, for supplies and in connection with the pearling industry, now almost dead.

4. Tucker: Australian colloquialism meaning food or provisions.

5. The children were no longer available as labourers to tend the garden.

6. Williams: her maiden surname, adopted from her father's first name, William, given him by the early missionary.

7. Later information revealed the estrangement of her parents; their separation no doubt accounted for some of Elsie's sensitivity to teasing by the other girls.

8. Some of the above discussion about menarche, menses, and babies took place in the early group sessions with the elder women who were all products of the dormitory system. They were bashful and embarrassed when I introduced these topics, and the discussion proceeded in whispered tones, interspersed with many quiet, girlish giggles. Some claimed they thought a 'bird' brought babies, and none could report how they allowed the knowledge of sex and pregnancy and delivery to come to their awareness.
Only one dormitory girl was remembered to have become pregnant out of marriage. She was allowed to stay at the Mission and have the child; the reputed father was sent to the mainland.

9. In the old part of the village was a corrugated iron dwelling in which three elderly women and one man resided. This might be called the 'old peoples home' of the community. The four inhabitants showed signs of marked senility.

10. Information given by an older person, probably of an age comparable to that of her mother, revealed that it was Lizzie, her mother, who left William, Elsie's father. Lizzie went to live with another man. This informant reported that Lizzie's parents disapproved of this, but her husband didn't care.

6
Elsie as a Wife

As near as could be ascertained, both by interview and observation, Elsie and her husband, Dick, had complemented each other in many useful ways. They were truly devoted. There were several areas where interpersonal difficulty might have developed and produced serious rupture in their relationship; however, through regard and respect for each other, the potential areas of difficulty seemed to have been resolved.

As stated earlier, Elsie was open, verbal, and comfortable in relating to Westerners. Her husband, Dick Roughsey, in the last ten years had achieved prominence in greater Australia, first as an artist and more recently through the publication of his own autobiography. He had become a member of several important councils that deal with various aspects of Aboriginal activities. As a result, he frequently visited various Australian cities. In addition, Dick, from time to time, had lived in mainland towns when he had held art shows or had been working on his writing. Elsie had joined him for varying periods, up to six months. This frequency of urban contact no doubt made them somewhat atypical of most of the island inhabitants.

Courtship and Wedding
Elsie and Dick, who was three years her senior, had known each other since childhood, both having been born on the island and raised in the dormitory system. They had not been 'promised' nor had been 'special friends'.[1] The idea that they should marry had been fostered by the fact that Elsie's older sister had married Dick's older brother. In their kinship way of relating they were already 'in-laws'. In addition, they were 'grannie' cousins.[2] Their parents and other relatives had suggested

to Dick that he should marry Elsie. So following the practice mentioned earlier, Dick had gone to the Missionary, who in turn had spoken to Elsie. To quote Elsie, 'I didn't especially like Dick and I don't think he was in love with me. I had a choice to make, but I never really said yes or no, although we were getting things ready for the marriage.

'We were married in the church. The wedding feast was so big. All kinds of relatives and friends came. There was much food to eat and everyone was quite happy. Although we had never known each other as special friends, everything went well. We are still happy.'

The Household
Until they moved into the new house in April of 1973, Elsie and Dick had lived on the same plot of ground, an area about 20 metres square. It was in the centre of village activity, by the main well and by the dancing ground. Four different structures had represented home. At first they had a shelter of old iron under what has become a large and lovely mango tree. Next they had a hut made of stringy bark,[4] and then a hut of iron. In 1970 their dwelling consisted of two separate structures, built of corrugated iron, raised about half a metre off the ground. Each structure, about 3 by 6 metres, was used primarily for sleeping. Elsie's three older sons and her nephew slept in one, and she and her husband and three younger children in the other. Except for cots and a table, there was little else besides old suitcases and boxes with clothes in them. My description is what I saw from 'peeping in' as I was never actually asked inside.

As was typical for most families, the Roughsey's used the inside of the house primarily for sleeping, dressing, and storing possessions. On very hot nights, some slept outside. Most activities, such as cooking, eating, laundering, or just yarning would take place in the yard. It was natural for Elsie to entertain in the yard, which was bare except for a blanket or two used for sitting. The mango tree furnished shade. Elsie and all the people appeared to be quite comfortable sitting on the ground. No doubt the outside living was a product of the traditional life, the warm climate and the small dwellings.

Behind the dwelling was a latrine (closed pan type). The entire plot was surrounded by a wire fence, topped with barbed wire. Their dwelling was typical of those in the village.

Elsie explained that during a recent six-month period, while she and the family were away from the island, most of their possessions had 'disappeared', and there had been no money available to replace many items. That was why there was so little in the house.

Marital Life

In reflecting about the early months of their marriage, Elsie thought they had been trying for both herself and her husband. She said, 'When I was young I didn't know about love for a man, of how the body works. I sort of understood you were to do something with a husband. The older girls would tease the younger ones. I was completely ignorant about sex, but I gradually understood. When I got married I wasn't brave with him. I could hardly speak to him, although he tried to talk to me. For me, the first experience was very unpleasant.[5] I knew women did this sort of thing with their husbands, but I never felt happy about having sex. I never was for it too much, not even now. I'd have a restless night after a relation, my back would ache, and I'd feel sick and tired the next day. My husband understood this; we'd talk about it. He would help me by not being demanding. No, I don't feel ashamed about sex, or about telling you. I think some find happiness and pleasure in it; I know it's not wrong. It's not disgusting, but I felt that way. I'd get no relaxation out of the act. My husband has never expressed anger or sadness over this; I don't think it is too important to him either.

'We people don't do much in the way of showing affection, like kissing, except when a near relative leaves. I see white people kiss more often. Dick and I have lived with each other so long; we are contented in the way we live and love each other. Devotion is real firm between the two of us.' (This is certainly revealed by the loving and warm way she would speak about her spouse, especially when she would refer to him by her 'pet' name, Dicky.)

'We have no reason to suspect each other. I know other couples are unfaithful. I couldn't do anything foolish with another person and neither could Dick. I often wonder how other husbands and wives do such things and continue to live with each other. It's my sense of values. I think Dick has the same set of values not to hurt me and the children.

'My first pregnancy just happened. We planned for the second child and for the two we lost. I had thought it was a safe period right after the monthly. If you wanted a baby it was most likely to happen a week or two after the monthly.' (This fact she claimed she had discerned from her observations of her own experiences; certainly a remarkably accurate conclusion.)

After the last pregnancy (six living children, two dead), Elsie and her husband had gone to one of the Mission nursing sisters and asked if there were not some way of preventing further pregnancies. When given the information about oral contraception, she immediately had accepted the pill. This openness and readiness to seek this type of information is in marked contrast to the attitude of many others on the island, which will be dealt with in a later section.

After being on the oral contraceptive for about a year, Elsie had developed amenorrhea and thought the pill had not worked. She had sought medical attention only to find that she had a gynaecological condition (ovarian cyst) that required surgery. During the operation, tubal ligation was performed, so that pregnancy was no longer a possibility. She had felt much better physically, and had liked the idea of having no more children. In 1970, she continued to have periods. Three years later, she reported that she no longer had her 'monthly' and was not aware of any symptoms associated with its cessation.[6]

How had this couple interacted in other areas of living? The handling of money is always an important area for any pair. During the early years of their marriage, Dick had worked both at the Mission and on the mainland in many capacities: carpenter, policeman, crewman on a boat, and cattle worker, to name only a few. He had not made much money, and Elsie had not 'bothered' with it. In more recent years, since he had developed his art and had a greater income, at least periodically, she claimed that she had taken care of the money. When her husband had money, 'He might spend it on things to give the children or race off to buy what he wants. I keep control of it. He knows I can look after

Elsie and Dick Roughsey in front of their new home in 1973

money better.' In many ways she believed she was 'boss'. For example, when Dick wanted to 'go bush', if she did not think it was a good time, he would not go.

Elsie related that it was she who had stimulated her husband to develop his art and had continued to motivate him in his career. She continued to assist him by doing some of the less skilled tasks involved. His work now takes him away from the island for varying periods of time. She felt that she was accustomed to his being away, although she certainly missed him when he was not home. For two periods, when he had been away for a number of months, she and the children had joined him, and all of them had lived near a small city. Needless to say, this was not only an exciting period for the family, but one that had presented them with many situations requiring judgment and adaptation. (See Chapter 9.)

There were ways in which Dick showed his dependency on Elsie for her judgment. This was illustrated by an interaction between the two. On one occasion, while Elsie and I were meeting, Dick appeared in a state of confusion and depression. There were many factors involved, but the crucial issue at the moment was whether or not he could get off the island to attend a meeting in Sydney. Several days previously he had told the Missionary that he was supposed to attend a meeting. When the Missionary raised a question about the absence of the plane ticket that was to have been provided by the sponsoring organization, Dick had interpreted this as lack of permission to leave the island. Elsie suggested to her husband a number of ways to obtain the information about the plane ticket, while stating that obviously one cannot fly without a reservation. After she had explained this to him in several different ways, he was able to come out of his confusion and depression and take the necessary steps. After Dick had left, Elsie stated, 'See how I have to explain things to him and push him. He has had a lot more contact with Europeans than I, but I often have to clear up his misunderstanding.' Dick had a great deal of social poise, ability for creative activity, and capacity for original thought, but Elsie certainly had been a positive force in his life.

As will be seen, the area where they seemed to have failed together, at least so far, was in helping their elder sons to become more reliable and independent individuals. A trait that both Dick and Elsie shared was that of exceeding generosity, and inability to say no to demands made on them. Therefore, they had not been successful in disciplining their children: they had been reluctant to displease anyone, even their own children.

In spite of their marriage having been initiated on somewhat shaky grounds — that is, not having been quite right-head, having had difficulty in sexual adjustment, and Dick's having protracted absences from the island because of his work — the Roughsey's relationship had been warm and stable. They had negotiated the vicissitudes of marriage. Furthermore, they (especially Dick) had begun to move out into the greater Australian society without any significant disruption in their relationship.

Notes

1. 'Special friend': a term used by Elsie meaning an intimate love relationship, comparable to the European's 'going steady' or being 'engaged'.
2. A 'grannie' or tribal cousin: terms derived from the practice of grandfathers calling men other than blood relatives 'brother'. The children of the tribal brothers were referred to as tribal cousins.
3. Dick and Elsie's marriage was not quite, but almost, correct as a right-head union.
4. Stringy bark: the bark of Eucalyptus tetradonta, a predominant tree species in northern Australia; the bark is tough and may be flattened by curing in hot sand. The inner surface is used as the 'canvas' in bark painting.
5. In my group discussion with the women it was reported that it might take couples several weeks before they had sexual relations.
6. None of the post-menopausal women reported any difficulty during 'the change of life'. Lack of menopausal symptoms was confirmed by the nursing sisters. Apparently these Aboriginal women accepted the menopause as a natural occurrence and nothing to complain about.

7
Elsie as a Mother

My first introduction to any of Elsie's progeny was to her only grand-child, a girl of about two and a half. She called the little girl over to her from a group of about eight women and children who were around the village well that stood about 12 metres from the fence of her yard. She was obviously both fond and proud of the child, whom she af-fectionately pulled down to her lap. Elsie then pointed out the child's mother, one of the young Kaiadilt women by the well: 'My oldest son got the girl pregnant while both were working on the mainland. Parents are very strict on the island and there is big trouble if a girl gets pregnant here. If it happens away from the island, well — we have to accept it. My son and the Kaiadilt girl don't even talk now; don't think of getting married.'

It is pertinent to point out that this was not an unusual situation on the island, where there was a low rate of marriage, and a high rate of births outside of marriage. In 1970, of the thirty-four women, aged 18 to 29, only fourteen were married. However, thirteen of the twenty unmarried in this age group had had one or more children.

Elsie explained that when a young couple who wish to marry are of a kinship group that would make it a right-head marriage, the parents are pleased, especially if the young man is a hard worker. From Elsie's point of view, a right-head marriage is desirable to carry on the kinship tradition; in addition the sons-in-law and daughters-in-law are more likely to respect and 'look after' their parents-in-law.

At times when a very young girl is impregnated by a young man of the right kinship group, marriage may not result; but the young parents may live together in the family of one of the grandparents. This gives them time to see if they are going to like each other enough to marry eventually.

On the other hand if a proposed marriage of a young couple would result in a wrong-head union, frequently a big fight could develop between the parents and other kin. The girl's parents might call the boy all sorts of derogatory names, while the boy's family might say she is 'no good'. This dissension might go on for months and possibly result in fighting with boomerangs or *nulla nullas*. The degree of the parental disagreement depends upon how threatened they feel by a non-kinship union. There is security in keeping the extended family viable in the expectation of mutual support in material and political matters. Whether or not the couple eventually married depended on the intensity of their desire to do so in the face of their relatives' violent disapproval. Usually the disagreeing families eventually accept the marriage.

Should a girl become pregnant while working or visiting on the mainland, the parents accept it as just 'one of those things that happens'. In fact, it would seem that this may be preferred. To quote Elsie, 'Someone somewhere gave the girl a baby, and no one knows anything about the boy, his bad traits or bad family'. The anonymity of the father apparently allowed for non-ambivalent acceptance of the baby into the family.

Elsie had six living children, five sons who in 1970 were aged twenty-two, twenty-one, sixteen, eight, and six and a daughter aged thirteen. She had a stillborn daughter and a boy who died at the age of eighteen months. None of the elder sons then, or three years later, showed the slightest inclination for marriage. Elsie said that this avoidance of marriage by the young folk was a result of the 'new ways' and not of the traditional life. In fact, she claimed that in former times, refusal to marry one's promised might have resulted in tribal retribution in the form of death, killed either by weapons or by sorcery.

However, she and Dick had not promised any of their children: 'If we had, we could have had a lot of heartache and trouble. We left our children to choose their own. If children are promised and then want to marry someone else when they grow up, there are a lot of family fights, like I told you about.'

Pregnancy and Childbirth

Elsie gave a good description of the events that she and apparently most island women of her generation had experienced during pregnancies: 'when a woman is pregnant, at first she fights a lot with her husband. Lots of things make her feel angry, growl, fight. Folks say "that husband and wife fight too much, going to have baby".[1] Later she cools down and then the headaches and vomiting start. Old people say *mongardai,* its the baby. If the husband would go hunting he'd tie twine on his right arm. That's good luck.[2] He was sure to come back with what he went for. The baby gives the father good tucker. Everytime he goes to sea, he's got to tie his arm. Everyone is happy for the parents. During the last months of pregnancy something wonderful is happening to the man. When the woman is far along she gets very touchy; fights with a big baby in her tummy.

'I had Lardil women help when I had my first two children, there were not nursing sisters here then. When the first one was coming, I was in bed two or three days. It was hard to know how to have a baby. Day and night the house was full of women. On the third night the baby was born. My mother was with me during my first two deliveries. She would chant over my tummy to wake up the baby inside. They had songs to make the baby move. Only the old people knew the chants. I think old Lettie Jacobs is the only one left who knows them. In addition to the help from my mother's chanting, many women helped, including Mrs McCarthy, the Missionary's wife. Lettie cut the cord. My mum only supervised.

'Sisters-in-law are not allowed around, as it would be like sharing the same bed as the brother. Brothers are not to have the shame. It has something to do with respectability, although he is proud his sister is having a baby.

'Only after a month does the new mother bathe herself and the baby,[3] and go to see her own father. The father kisses his daughter and grandchild. Later the wives of her brothers and her cousin-brothers take the baby to be seen by them, while the mother must stand some 10 feet (3 metres) away.'[4]

Elsie had her first five deliveries (including the two who died) in the village. However, her daughter was born at the Mission hospital and her two younger sons were delivered at a hospital on the mainland, as Elsie had developed hypertension during these last two pregnancies. It was only when she gave birth to her first son, Mervin, that her husband had been around. At the time of the deliveries of the other children, he had always been working elsewhere. She claimed that she had never minded his absences, because she knew he had to be off the island to make money. The fact that she mentioned this, only to negate it, would seem to indicate that she did, indeed, have some feelings about this.

Early Child-Rearing Practices

Although Elsie did not have too much to say about her early relations with her children, she did relate some interesting practices. In order to have her children grow fast and strong, and rest well, when each was about three weeks old, either her mother or Lettie Jacobs would place the infant in the early morning dew and chant over the child. This custom was to help make the child healthy.

Another traditional practice that Elsie carried out was that *jungue*, or navel custom. Her description of it is as follows: 'When the navel (umbilical) cord falls off the child, it is given to the mother's father or the mother's uncle if the father is dead. He wraps it in a cloth. The mother wears this around her neck. The child then grows to be big and strong as he can smell part of his own body as well as his mother's body. She wears this for two or three months. When she is sure the baby is going to be good by sleeping while the mother works, it is safe for her to take the *jungue* packet from around the neck and leave it by the side of the baby.'

Elsie's father had wrapped the cord for all her children, except her youngest. By that time her father had died, so her brother, Colin, had arranged the packet. Another part of the *jungue* custom would not take place until several years later, perhaps not until the child was five or six. The second ceremony was one of gift-giving. It was held when the parents and relatives felt they had collected sufficient gifts to make a proper ceremony in order to 'square-off'.[5]

At the second ceremony, the child would be seated on a blanket and many gifts would be heaped around him by the uncles and cousin-brothers. These would include such things as sheets, trousers, shirts, flour, sugar, soap, dishes, and buckets, A *coolamon* (a curved carrying tray made of bark) and a head-band would be given to the mother and a hair-belt to the father. When all the gifts had been given, the mother and her sisters would carry away the presents in the blanket. Then another blanket would be spread out and the parents of the child would place gifts on it for the relatives who had given the presents to the child.

Regarding their toilet training, Elsie had this to say, 'I would sit my children on the pottie when I saw them pushing and grunting. I guess I started this when they were eight or nine months old.[6] I didn't nurse them often, only when they needed to have a suck to make them sleep. Then I could get on with my work.'

Elsie said, 'It wasn't hard for me to train my children to be nice and loving, and not to be cheeky with those they played with. I was easy with them, because my father used to say "don't hit children, be kind to them".' She claimed that in the olden days parents didn't hit their children. But if, perchance, some parents had abused a child, he would be taken by the grandparents to live with them.

The claim of Elsie's about the ease and success in rearing her offspring as young children was at variance with the problems that were now her major concern.

A Mother Worries About Her Children

During my first visit, in spite of the amount of time I spent with Elsie and her husband around their house, in the village and in the Mission area, her children (except for her twelve-year-old daughter) were like shadows in the background. As individuals they were unknown to me; they faded into the group of young people. However, I heard a great deal about them from their mother, especially her concerns. Their elusiveness was demonstrated the first morning that I sat with Elsie on the blanket in her yard. Earlier Elsie had raked leaves and trash into piles. Periodically she called out to the elder sons, who were in the house, to come burn the trash, but they never appeared.

Elsie remarked, 'children are more spoiled now than when we lived in the Mission. It's the softness of the parents. I talk and talk, but my husband doesn't back me up. It's more laziness than disobedience. Most fathers think it's the mother's job to correct children.

'My two oldest sons do odd jobs, like unload boats, clean wells, carry stones. Mervin is good with his hands, but he's not interested in crafts like his father. I tell them they have to go ask for work, not just sit and wait for someone to come to them. They worked for a while helping to build the new houses, but the boss said all they did was kid around and tell stories, so he had to let them go.

'I know I spoil them; if they aren't here at mealtime they eat whenever they get home. Maybe if I'd let them go without a meal, they'd be there on time. I don't know how to be hard, except when they break the law; then I really fuss. The boys have gone to gaol for stealing food and clothing. Other boys do worse things, but they fight the police so they aren't put in gaol, but my boys say "all right" and go to gaol.[7] I think most of their misdeeds are the fault of other boys; they put my sons up to doing these things.

'Yesterday Raymond went to church. His father conducted the service. The other boys said a nasty "no" to the suggestion that they go. When I got home, I found money missing from my bag. They took it to use for gambling. The boys have a don't-care feeling; they only do what they want.'

Some days later, when Dick was depressed about certain other matters, he said, 'I just want to get away from my grown sons. I want them to go to another island to fend for themselves. I just don't know what to do with them.' Elsie interrupted and pointed out that he always walked away from them when there was an argument, and she was the one who had to 'growl' at the boys.

Elsie claimed that their sons started 'getting into trouble' in 1968 when the family was living in Cairns for some months, and that they had given her no trouble while they were growing up. But then she went on to tell how when they got to be sixteen, the school-leaving age, she started missing things from the house. They were probably using household objects to support their gambling. As far as I could ascertain, this type of stealing was either ignored, or dealt with by Elsie's 'fussing'.

An excellent illustration of how Elsie and her husband were caught in a dilemma to a great extent of their own making was shown by their sleeping accommodations in 1970. The parents and the six-year-old son slept on mats, while the daughter and older boys all slept on cots. Elsie remarked, 'Dick even bought a bed and gave it to Mervin'.

Elsie mentioned that on the mainland she had seen European boys look after themselves. However, she wanted to keep her boys on the island, where they are less likely to get into trouble, and the boys did not want to leave: 'They aren't interested in marriage either. I wanted Raymond to marry the girl who had his baby, but he didn't want to, and now she has had another child by another man. My nephew, who lives with us, is a silly boy. They do a bit of joking about girls. I do notice my oldest boy creeps away at night.'

Elsie's only daughter, Eleanor, aged twelve, was frequently with her mother, or would come and go as we were chatting; and she was in-cluded in the fishing trip and other activities. Her dress and grooming were untidy. Elsie said, 'It is my duty to keep Eleanor under my eye and away from sex. I teach her the right way. If girls would only tell their mothers the truth it would avoid a lot of trouble. Often truth only comes out in arguments'. In spite of her philosophy that mothers should be told the truth, for Elsie the complementary notion that mothers should state the facts to their daughters did not appear to apply. She had not broached the subject of menarche or other facets of sexual life to her daughter. She knew that it was about time that she should, and she denied any possibility that her daughter already might have learned such information from other girls. The idea that she should discuss sexual matters with her daughter was a change in at-titude from what she had experienced in her Mission upbringing; however, putting the idea into action was a step that she could not bring herself to take.

The whereabouts of the six-year-old son was never apparent. Perhaps Elsie summed up the problems she was experiencing with her children by saying, 'Parents have slackened on looking after their children. I think parents force children into trouble instead of being good and responsible. Why can't we help them? Dick and I grew up better than our children. No matter how much we tell them to work, and ask them to help with the food money when they get a little work, they do nothing. They can eat the family's food, but not one boy helps us. Dick and I go to church and are good Christians. Dick was home most of the time when Mervin and Raymond were young. Then he was away a good deal until the past six years,[8] so for ten years they were mainly my responsibility. Is this why Dick is not firm enough with the boys?'

While the Roughsey's sons were unknown to me during my first trip to the island, during the 1973 visit while living with the family, the sons became less like shadows. My observations verified Elsie's previously expressed concerns. The second son, Raymond, was not on the island as he had been on the mainland for a month working at a cattle station. However, Mervin, aged twenty-five, and Kevin, aged nineteen, were living at home and did nothing that could be called work.

A typical day for these two young men consisted of their staying in bed late, then looking around to see if there were any porridge or damper left from breakfast. Then they would disappear, often with several other young men of comparable age. Where and how they spent their days could only be guessed. In the early evening, and occasionally at noon, they would reappear to find what might be available in the way of food. Once Mervin sat down at the table with Nancy Waxler and me. The three of us could manage only the most stilted conversation. He finished eating first and excused himself as he got up from the table. As night came on, Mervin and Kevin would again disappear, not to be seen until the following day when they finally got out of bed.

One evening Elsie, in a very kind way, asked Mervin to get up early to start an outside fire to cook porridge, as the wood stove would not work. The smoke stack was clogged with soot and there was no fuel for the primus stove. But Mervin did not appear. After an unsuccessful attempt bs Nancy to get an outside fire started, eleven-year-old Basil accomplished this. Needless to say, the younger children were late for school that day.

Except when in school, Eleanor, in 1973, spent most of her time around the house and did many of the chores for her mother. She would make the tea, wash clothes and the like. While she would have little to say, she tended to stay around us adults and always joined Nancy and me in our nightly star gazing. This was her last year in school, but she had no idea about how she would occupy her time after graduation. She had her sixteenth birthday while we were there. Apparently, it was not customary to have any sort of celebration either in the home or in school for such an event. I had an extra dress that I had purchased in Mt Isa which I gave her as Nancy and I sang 'Happy Birthday'. Eleanor looked non-plussed.

Eleanor, according to her mother, had shown no interest in boys. She was defenseless against the teasing of Basil, her eleven-year-old brother. Her mother would tell her to stand up for herself, but she was too intimidated by his aggressiveness. In contrast, nine-year-old Duncan would fight back. On one occasion, Basil's teasing of his sister became so intolerable to Elsie that she took a broomstick to him. This was only momentarily effective in stopping his behaviour.

At one point, both Elsie and Dick attempted to cajole to the two elder sons into doing some painting, for which both have some talent. This ended with sons slipping off with their pals. About this time, Elsie pointed out that the boy next door was chopping wood, but in a 'bad humour'. I said that least he was doing it and wondered if she were afraid to put her sons in a bad humour. She denied this, relating how several years ago she had used a stick on Mervin when he had drunk 'metho' (methylated spirits or methyl alchohol) and claimed that he had not drunk spirits since then.

Another illustrative episode of Elsie's problem with her sons, and her inability to do anything but comply with a request, concerned the absent Raymond. She had expressed fear of his hurting himself while working at a station, since he had had no experience riding horses. Soon thereafter, she received a wire from him sent from Mt Isa, requesting $60.00 to return to Mornington (one-way airfare was $43.00). Although Elsie had only $63.00 in her account at the Mission office, she immediately wired the money Raymond requested. The fact that Elsie was to leave the island two days hence to go to Sydney did not cause her to hesitate in all but depleting her account. But Raymond did not arrive back on the next two planes, so Elsie left without knowing his actual whereabouts. But she was correct: when Raymond finally returned a week later, he said he had hurt his shoulder in falling from a horse. As far as I could ascertain, the injury had not been serious enough for him to seek medical attention.

Elsie appeared to have chronic anxiety about her older sons. On one hand she wished they would leave the island and fend for themselves, but at the same time she had a need to have them with her so that she could come to their aid if they got into difficulty. 'I grew up all by myself,' Elsie said. 'I'm a good mother, but I spoiled them too much.'

What Elsie was expressing was the vagueness and contradictions she had experienced with her own parental role models. Her Aboriginal parents, perhaps in part due to their estrangement, were indistinct figures in her memory of the time prior to her residing in the Mission dormitory. She wondered who might have told her to go there prior to moving into it. From her report of her father's telling her, 'Don't hit them,' in reference to her own children, we can assume a permissive attitude on the part of whoever was around in her early childhood.

Then, at age seven, she came under the strict discipline of the dormitory where the Missionary and his wife were the dominant figures.

Regimentation was the *modus operandi;* no doubt necessary when only two people were in charge of fifty children. While the Mission surrogate parents were remembered with fondness, the discipline and rigidity imposed must have been experienced as something foreign. It was literally foreign, as it was from an entirely different culture.

It was evident that Elsie, Dick, and their contemporaries had internalized much of the training and values of the Mission. But this was superimposed on their earlier Aboriginal culture, which was particularly permissive with young children. The adults who were the products of the dormitory system had two disparate types of parental models; neither was sufficiently internalized to allow them to become free of conflict in the role of parents.

Notes

1. The freer expression of irritation at this time may reflect ambivalent feelings about the pregnancy, as well as offering an excuse to express other angry feelings. It was typical of these people to avoid showing irritation or anger; however, the pregnant state apparently gave licence to display these feelings.
2. This custom is still practiced to some extent.
3. Currently this practice has been shortened to one week.
4. This is another example of the kinship avoidance rules: a living out of the incest taboo.
5. 'Square-off': make an equitable distribution. This term also applied to a get-together after the death of someone. The relatives 'square-off' to make sure the dead one was well treated, as well as to make a fair distribution of any possessions.
6. I had thought this must have been a retrospective exaggeration; however, many of the other women reported similar bowel training practices of their children at a quite young age. This must have been successful as far as bowel training is concerned as I had never noticed a small child squatting to defecate. It was not uncommon to see children urinate wherever the impulse occurred, at least up to school age.
7. There were five Aboriginal men considered by the Islanders to be police. However, they are not police officers, but perform a monitoring function under the Aborigine Protection Act Regulations.
8. This was during the ten years that Dick was developing his artistic medium.

8
Elsie as the Aboriginal Traditionalist

Elsie, as well as most of the middle-aged people on the Island, had maintained a keen interest in the practices and beliefs from the Lardil tradition. Some of these have been recounted in the preceding chapters. Elsie tended to romanticize the past, as well as to contradict herself. For example: 'Traditional government was better than white man's. If one did something wrong, he would be beaten with boomerangs by five or six men. The people were taught to be kind to each other, not mean!'

When she would launch into a story, at times I got the distinct feeling that she was making it up as she went along; however, she would end the tale in such a way as to make it a complete legend. Until soon after her third son had been born, Elsie had felt no especial curiosity about the legends and traditions of her tribe. She realized then that not only would they be lost for her own children, but that they would make good stories to tell other children. So she set about collecting the old legends from her father, her uncles and her cousins. She hoped that one day she would write down the tales for a children's book. This interest of her's coincided with the time that her husband had begun experimenting with his artistic work. According to her, it was she who had urged him to use the traditional symbols and legends as a background for his paintings.

Corroboree
Elsie and Dick, as well as others, were particularly interested in maintaining the traditional song and dance ceremony; that is, the corroboree, in which legends are enacted. This traditional mode of artistic expression had been dying out as tribal influences faded and the young people turned to European styles of dancing. However, because

their dance groups had begun having success performing before audiences in various Australian towns and cities, there had been a resurgence of interest in the corroboree.

Elsie said that legends to be danced come to people in their dreams. When the dreamer wakes, he makes up a story, a song, and a dance about his dream. Elsie gave the following example. A boy dreamed of a bush fire. All of a sudden a *garrd-garrd* bird smelled the bush fire and flew around it. He was looking for prey, such as lizards, that would be driven out by the fire. After having this dream, the boy would tell the story and make up a poem about the *garrd-garrd* birds sitting on posts ready to swoop down upon their prey. In the dance they would imitate the hovering of the birds and their swooping down. Another dance was called the brolga dance. Someone would dream about the brolga, a large bird also called native companion, and introduce it into a dance. In this both men and women would act like the bird. They would imitate how he eats, how he walks around, and also the sounds the bird makes.

It was considered unusual for a woman to have a corroboree dream. However, Elsie reported the following: 'I dreamed I saw a bush fire. I called out and a lot of people went and put out the fire. It left a lot of black, burned places. Some men made motions like they were sweeping the black mess away. Then the next moment fresh green grass was shooting up.' She made up a dance to re-enact this dream.

In a full-dress corroboree, men wear hair-belts and dancing hats and often carry a bundle of leaves. They decorate their bodies with ochre paint and also feathers, collected from cockatoos, brolgas, or other local birds. The dancing-hat is conical in shape, is made of bark tied together with a string of human hair. Rhymthmic accompaniment to the dance is provided by hitting boomerangs together, by special clapping sticks or by the drone of a didgeridoo (drone pipe).

In spite of the renewed interest in the corroboree dancing, the middle-aged people were always concerned that the younger people would neglect this tribal dance in favour of Western dancing. This was rather dramatically illustrated one Saturday evening when Elsie, Dick, and I walked down to the village dancing ground expecting to find a corroboree in progress. Instead we found two groups of young people dancing: one group was doing their variation of the hula to the accompaniment of a drum and two guitars, while a short distance away another crowd of even younger folk were 'twisting' to music from a record player. I have never seen such acute despair on the part of any two individuals. Dick frantically called for his older brother; who immediately appeared with a headdress and other trappings worn during a corroboree. All three were exceedingly distressed and dismayed. They could not even allow themselves the pleasure of

watching the imported dancing (which was being done very well); so we
quickly said 'goodnight', while they went home muttering, 'We must
do everything to preserve our own dances.'

Kinship and Taboos

The elaborate kinship system of the Lardil was manipulated many
times for convenience. This, in part, is the difference between the ideal
and the real. There had been perhaps as many wrong-head as right-head
marriages even prior to the advent of the Mission, which distorted the
kinship marriage line. The women reported that there had been
probably no more than six to eight right-head marriages between the
dormitory residents. However, maintaining and re-creating kinship
rules of marriage and some of the associated taboos had continued to be
of importance among the people.

As stated previously, Elsie and Dick's marriage was a wrong-head
marriage, but not very wrong. Elsie knew her own genealogy and that of
her extended family as well as that of most of the Lardil people. All
continued to use English derivatives of the kinship designations when
speaking to each other, such as, auntie, mother-in-law, father-in-law,
and cousin-brother. Uncles were frequently called father, as this
showed more respect. For example, Elsie called her father's half-
brother, Gully Peters, father.

According to Elsie, as soon as a girl reached puberty, she and her
brothers and cousin-brothers were not permitted to speak to each other
directly, much less touch each other.[1] They could send messages by way
of a third party, such as a parent or younger child. Elsie thought that
this avoidance showed 'love and respect'. These taboos in all
probability had been developed to minimise sexual encounter, but
characteristically Elsie avoided the sexual implications.

Elsie said that there were seven men in the village who were her
cousin-brothers. She mentioned that even now she tended not to speak
to them directly, but she certainly spoke directly to her blood brother as
I observed many times. At one time a brother would not sit next to his
sister's husband. If one of them wanted some of the other's tobacco, it
would have to be passed by a third person.

If a husband touched one of his brother's wives (his sister-in-law)
there would be a big fight. But upon the husband's death, the next
younger brother had first rights to take the widow as a wife. Since the
first husband was frequently considerably older than his promised wife,
a younger brother or other man might be much more sexually attractive
to the woman. However, Elsie claimed that an older man was preferred
as he was a much better provider and protector. Although in traditional
times the husband had always been boss, he and his wife would quarrel.

This quarrel would be ignored by the family group unless the husband became too cruel. Then there would be a big fight with the woman's father, grandfather, brothers, and cousin-brothers fighting the husband. Boomerangs and *nulla nullas* might be resorted to.

Totem

Elsie had this to say about this traditional concept: 'Totem means something that belongs to you, it's sacred. My mother's totem, or *jildreed,* was the dingo. If a dingo corroboree is to be sung and played, I must join in with all my mother's brothers and sisters. When I married Dick, I took on his totem, *goobalathalden.* This Lardil word means "rough seas". That's how we have Roughsey as our last name.[2]

'Some of the sacred things of an Aboriginal were secret and not to be touched or seen by women or young men. They were to be kept secret by the elders.' Perhaps the fact that the *jildreed* was part of secrets kept by the male elders of the tribe accounts for my being unable to obtain much information concerning this aspect of the traditional life from the present day Lardil women. The elders did not pass on their secrets.

Dreams

Dreams have always been important in the Aboriginal traditional life. To Elsie, the content of a dream had prophetic meaning or was to be danced in a corroboree. She told several dreams that had prophetic content. These dreams did not seem to be necessarily Elsie's dreams, but reflected symbolic meanings particular to the Lardil people. Examples were:

1. in a dream someone was hit on the head, symbolizing that someone had speared a dugong or a turtle;
2. if in a dream someone got hurt, a big fight would take place days later;
3. if one dreamt that one was in a dinghy full of salt water, but was not drowning, and could see oneself coming to shore, this would be interpreted that someone very close to the dreamer was sick but would not die.

Elsie, herself, had several dreams in which it seemed to be pitch black, and flying foxes were flying over her house from the west to the east (heaven is in the east). One of her cousin-brothers had the flying fox as his totem. Soon after she had dreamt this recurrent theme, the man had died and she no longer dreamed of the flying foxes.[3]

Elsie went on to tell the following story in relationship to a dream. Her mother had died in the morning and was buried the same evening. That very night Elsie had dreamt that a great light came from the west over her house. It was from a magic stone. In the dream she had put an empty tin can in the window to catch the light so that it would hit the tin can and bounce back rather than hit her. She did not want the light to hit her body for fear that it might hurt her. The dream conveyed the idea that when the light from the magic stone hit the tin can, it bounced back to the grave where her mother was buried. That same night Jackson Jacobs, who was her mother's favourite nephew, was on the mainland. He was lying under a tree at a cattle station. All of a sudden he could feel the shadow of her mother, whom he knew as Aunt Lizzi. He thought, 'Here I am awake, but I see this figure, something must be wrong.' Then his Aunt Lizzi (who was Elsie's mother) said, 'I'm dead, but I will give you one present which will cure anyone when they are sick.' So, she gave him a magic or lucky stone.

Elsie went on to say that Jackson Jacobs still has the lucky charm with him, and that it will cure any sickness. In fact, recently, when her legs had been hurting her very badly, Elsie had gone to see Jackson, whom she calls son-in-law and his wife, Enid, whom she calls daughter-in-law. She told them how her legs hurt so much, and then Jackson touched her foot and sang a healing song. Her legs then felt better; not so numb and cold. She could not catch the words of the song. She thought that the song had lasted for three or four minutes and could have come from Dreamtime. The fact that she still complained of numbness in her lower back and the posterior aspects of her legs did not seem to weaken the idea that he had the power to cure any sickness.

Elsie: Illness, Magic and Cures

At the time of my second visit to the island, Elsie was complaining of a feeling of discomfort and numbness involving the lower part of the lumbar area of her back, the sacrum, and the backs of both legs. I performed a neurological examination on her. There seemed to be a loss of ability to discriminate certain sensations in her area of numbness. I recommended that she avail herself of a more complete medical-neurological examination when she went to Sydney. She had suffered from this complaint for the past two years, and had been taking 'pain pills' given to her by the nursing sisters. Once, when she was in Cairns, she had made an abortive attempt to get help, but had never followed through by having the x-rays that the doctor had recommended. Coincidentally, the day after I had done the neurological examination, she reported that she felt much better.

My colleague, Dr Nancy Waxler, who accompanied me during my second visit to the island, was interested in learning what the people had to say about local individuals whom they considered to have been 'mad'. Certainly, from the descriptions given by Elsie and others, the 'mad' ones could be considered psychotic in the technical sense. In relating the madness of several people, Elsie in retrospect wondered whether this could have been the result of sorcery. She thought that sorcery was still being practised, although she had never seen it: thus, if one were to get sick, there were two choices. One was to go to the hospital, and the other one was to go to a native songman. If the songman was a kinship relative, one did not have to pay him, as this was part of the services provided by the extended kinship group.

Other informants who spoke of sorcery said that it was supposed to cause death, and that madness came from lack of sex. However, Elsie thought that sorcery could cause madness as well as death. She gave as an example that in the old days people tended to eat their meat half-raw. If someone complained that the meat was too raw and that it should be cooked again, this might have offended the donor of the meat. Then, at some future time, the donor might chant and put sorcery on the offender who had complained about the meat. Perhaps, then, as much as a year or more later, the victim might develop madness or might die.

Elsie told a story that happened when she was a young woman, not yet married. The story concerned her Uncle Henry who was very sick. Another uncle, Old Jimmy Dugong, came along with a crowbar needle that was used to sew sacks. He put the needle straight into the area where the pain was (right lower quandrant of abdomen). He did not sterilize the needle or anything. It went the whole way in an all of a sudden it came out the back of Uncle Henry. Uncle Henry supposedly had a hair-belt inside of him, and the needle relieved the pressure from the hair-belt. The amazing thing according to Elsie, was that this was the first time that she had seen a black man use a needle, or in fact, had seen anyone use a needle. However, she said that soon thereafter a Red Cross nurse came to the island and started giving needles to cure people.

Another healing story of Elsie's concerned an event involving her husband, Dick. Years ago, he had been making a dugout canoe way out in the bush when he cut his kneecap. She screamed, and his brother, Kenny, who was a songman, came and took the axe, and put it against the big cut, and squeezed the skin together, and sang one of the healing chants. Then, all of a sudden, the big gash closed and they walked home. She said that the healing chants came from 'dreamland', and were known only to the songman. She thought that if such an accident were to happen in the village today, she might do the same thing; however, others would rush the wounded individual to the hospital.

Elsie explained that some cures are brought about by certain local remedies. For example, when one boils a certain type of grass in a drum, the liquid becomes tea-colored. One should throw away the grass and take a bath in the liquid; it makes one feel so clean and fresh.

Recently, Elsie said, she had taken such a bath after the pills that the nursing sisters had given her had failed to relieve her back discomfort; and the bath made her feel so much better.

Also, there is a little tree that has white berries on it, which they call a woollen tree. When one takes several sticks from the tree and scrapes the bark from them, the water it is boiled in will turn green. The green liquid can be used to cure any illness. Anyone can make it, it need not be a special person, such as a songman. Elsie then remembered a relative who some years ago had been 'mad'. The songman had not helped the madness, so she was sent to a hospital on the mainland, where she remained for a year and a half. When she came back to the island she was much better, but not cured. Then someone gave her some of this green liquid to drink and this is what really cured the madness.

A common belief concerned a disorder called *malgri*.[4] This condition is characterized by acute abdominal pain and swelling. The victim may also vomit, groan, and writhe in pain. There is no diarrhoea, but instead marked constipation. In fact, in some cases, the description of the condition sounds like a severe case of constipation. *Malgri* is believed to develop from handling or eating land food before going into the sea. To prevent this, any trace of odour from land food must be thoroughly removed from the skin with sand and water, or the evil spirit of the *malgri* will enter the belly. This is not considered a medical illness like 'gastro',[5] but a condition in which the traditional laws have been violated, so that a tribal doctor or songman is the one to be consulted. He cures by a healing chant, and by rubbing his axillary sweat over the abdomen of the affected person and blowing over the area. This exorcises the spirit of the sea serpent, or whatever totem is in the stomach. The person then has a bowel movement and has no more pain.

Elsie related that one of her sons, when he was about six, had just had dinner (meat, damper, butter, and jelly) before going for a swim. He developed a bad pain in his tummy. She immediately said that the sea hawk or other totem had gotten into him, so she took him to one songman who sang and rubbed smell from under his arm on the boy's tummy; but he was not better. She continued, 'I took him to Old Lem; he did the same, and he was still in terrible pain. Lem's wife even took soap and made a little stick and pushed it into his bottom, and that did not work. So, then I took him to Uncle Kenny, the best songman. He did not sing him, just put smell from under arm to Basil's tummy. He felt a lot better. Uncle Kenny blew his tummy again, and drove the *malgri* from him. Basil went to the toilet and was well again.'

I had learned about *malgri* early in my stay on the island. After having eaten land food before going fishing, Elsie indicated to me that I should thoroughly wash my hands and mouth with the drinking water that we had with us. I immediately did so; Elsie expected it.

In another story of *malgri*, Elsie told about a man named Adam, whose name she claims is coincidental and has nothing to do with the Bible. Adam and two other men were out hunting sea turtle. The water was calm, but way out at sea they saw waves coming; they wondered what the waves meant. Adam was trying to lift a turtle into the canoe when something grabbed him. When the men pulled Adam into the boat they found claw scratches. It was a sea hawk that had grabbed him. The canoe filled with blood, but the men sang the *malgri* song to take the hawk out of his body. Later when he went to the toilet, instead of having the usual bowel movement, he passed feathers. He was all right then.

While Elsie spoke of *malgri* as if she were convinced that there really is an evil spirit that causes the distress, she conceded that some of the women in the village take their children who have abdominal pain to the medical dispensary, and that the nursing sisters do cure them.

Elsie reported a number of other conditions in which traditional practices have been used to alleviate them. One she referred to as the *dami dami* custom. If a baby were small, or parts of the features seemed out of shape, the grandparents would squeeze the muscles and warm the skin. Recently her niece's baby was so small that they had had to do these magic things. If a fleshy part were too big, such as the ears, one would have to pinch the skin and to make a kissing sound with the lips all the time. If the buttocks were too large, one would have to hit them to make them small.

Elsie thought she had polio about twelve years ago. She had felt a stiffness in her back, her neck, and shoulders. The Mission's treatment did not make her better, so her brother put magic stones on her forehead. She went on to say, 'His wife, Carrie, was with me, as brothers are not to speak directly to their sister. He told Carrie that we may see queer things, like a man or a snake, but not to be afraid; it would be the magic power that would appear during the night and made me feel better. It was past midnight when Carrie and I heard something. There was a big rattle and noise of a snake under my bed. We both knew it was a snake, but didn't take any notice, like my brother said. We both went off to sleep, and the next morning I was as bright as anything. We knew my brother hadn't put anything under my bed; it was a doctor snake.' She told this in a self-conscious way, smiling, but serious.

Some of Elsie's cures were less dramatic. Her three younger children had had pains around their navels during the previous month. She wet her thumb with saliva and then put her thumb on their navels.

Gradually the pains went away. I suggested that possibly it was the attention and comfort they were getting from her as their mother that was important. She partly agreed, but claimed that she had seen her father do the same and she believed in the old ways.

Elsie appeared to enjoy relating these various tribal beliefs, legends, and cures. Her attitude was both serious and interested. However, at times I sensed that she was telling me some of this material because she thought I wanted to hear it, and she was being the obliging informant. She also seemed to believe most of the legends as if she did not dare to question them.

Notes

1. Brothers: term used to designate blood brothers as well as father's brother's son and mother's sister's son.
   Cousin-brothers: term used to designate father's sister's son or mother's brother's son.
2. It is questionable that in the traditional culture a woman assumed her husband's totem. The Mission initially gave English first names to the Islanders. Later they found it necessary to assign surnames; most of these are common English ones. However, several families have surnames which are derived from the translation of the family totem. Accordingly, Dick's two brothers also have the surname of Roughsey. Another surname of a family derived from their totem is Dugong.
3. It would be tempting to speculate about the symbolism and latent meanings of these dreams. However, I think it is more circumspect to accept Elsie's interpretations; as this was what her culture has imparted to her and was what she believed.
4. See John Cawte, *Medicine is the Law.* Honolulu, University Press of Hawaii, 1974, pp. 106-120, for his description of this 'culture bound' syndrome.
5. 'Gastro' or 'runny tummy' were the terms for diarrhoea. When an individual developed this condition medical attention was sought.

9

Elsie as a Social Person

Elsie's level of personal and social maturity will by now have become evident. She had negotiated the usual stages of life: childhood, marriage and motherhood. Some of the basic ingredients of her background were typical of the Christian Mission and of the dormitory system. At the same time, she was not entirely detached from the traditional past of her own tribe. Also, in recent years, she had had moderate contact with the white Australian community, albeit to a lesser extent than had her husband. What was Elsie like as a person in a specific community that had its own special transitional culture in the latter third of the twentieth century?

Certainly adjectives such as cooperative, friendly, generous, and intelligent all could be applied to Elsie. How she manifested these characteristics, and other facets of her personality could be observed in her daily life. She had grown up a Christian, and had lived out her Christianity in many ways. She reported what was apparently a religious conversion experience. In her words, 'When I was younger, I might not be too friendly, I'd fight, I wasn't being a good person.[1] One day I looked up into the sky; it was all blue without any clouds. All of a sudden little white clouds appeared and they made words like they were written by God's hand. Certain words meant hell-fire. From then on, I thought I should live a more decent life, not being crabby and fighting, but being friendly and serving others. Since then I have felt so much better. Most of the time now I stop others' fights and have so many friends.'

Elsie's Attitude Towards Fellow Islanders and Island Events

In 1970, Elsie's house was located near the centre of activity in the village, the well, where most came for water, and the dancing ground. She and Dick, through their open and generous natures, had made it a social centre. Not only did she like to yarn with everyone who came by, she actively encouraged social occasions in her yard. People stopped to borrow anything from fishing hooks to food or clothing. Somehow these things never were returned. As with their children, neither Dick nor Elsie could say no to anyone. 'Sometimes I feel my home is a serving station, a cafe, a resort. I get pleasure out of giving; I'm willing to share at the moment, but then I feel a bit angry.' She spoke of gathering some rare and valuable shells. She gave the best to a close friend on the mainland, but others wanted them, 'So I gave them all away. It worries me if I don't give things other people want. Dick is the same way. If he has a little money, he will buy ice cream and give it to all the children in the village.[2] He will spend money on others, but not on himself.' At that time I thought that Elsie had only herself (and Dick) to blame for feeling somewhat exploited for their generosity.

During my second visit, I was able to see that Elsie expected to be given to, or helped by others, to an equal or perhaps even greater degree. With most of her attention being focused on the manuscript, she devoted little time to household tasks. In addition, the chronic discomfort she felt in her lower back and legs was accentuated by physical activity. Therefore, her daughter Eleanor, Nancy and I, as well as Dick, usually prepared the available food. We made the tea and porridge, or heated canned meats. The Tim Roughseys, who lived next door, as well as others of the kinship group, were frequently asked to make damper, or cake, or to cook the bullock meat. She expected that I would contribute money for their efforts.

Traditionally, and currently, food and other possessions were ex-pected to be shared with the extended group. Such sharing had long been part of the Aboriginal social obligation. There were various hints that this type of obligation was beginning to arouse feelings of resent-ment in some. Factors contributing to this change of attitude could perhaps be explained by the gradual transition of the island economy from bartered goods to currency as the medium of exchange. Increasing contact with Europeans, who are more individualistic and who tend not to depend in the same manner on the extended family, could, by example, be weakening the willingness to give of one's possessions.

Elsie tended to make her requests by calling out to people as they walked by, especially if they were part of her extended family. Sometimes her requests did not bring the desired action. An example of this concerned the repair of the door to the shower room in the new house. The door had been blown off its hinges by a strong wind, and the layers of plywood were also separating. To shut the door while showering, it was necessary to pick it up and lean it across the opening. One morning, Elsie called out a number of times, over a period of several hours, to a nephew, who was one of the carpenters completing a house across the road, asking him to fix the door. The nephew neither acknowledged her requests nor showed any indication of coming to make the repairs.

In the interest of a more convenient shower arrangement, I walked over to the workmen and asked who was in charge. It was not the nephew. I told the man in charge about the problem with the door and wondered if it could be replaced. Within a brief period, several carpenters arrived and a new door was installed. I can only speculate as to whether this was an example where asking relatives to do favours was not necessarily effectivè as a kinship obligation, or that I, as guest, or perhaps representing white authority, obtained action, or that speaking to the boss was more effective than approaching one of the crew.

Elsie's attitudes concerning female matters and sexual life of the island women were of note. She recognized that there was considerable sexual promiscuity on the island, and that most girls were not virgins (I had to supply the word) at the time they married. She thought that the young girls tempted the men, and that they should be more careful and steady in their friendships until they were married. Elsie, thereby, placed the responsibility on the girl.

She was aware that extramarital affairs occur between individuals in her own age group. But she did not understand how a husband or wife would be willing to hurt each other in this way. When a very close woman friend had expressed great heartache over her spouse's infidelity, Elsie had attempted to help her by saying, 'You can't mend what is broken: you can only secure things by taking them to God.' When the villagers become aware of sexual misconduct among them, according to Elsie, 'At first there is a lot of talk, but then it is forgotten.'

Some of the younger women in the village were reluctant to be interviewed. In discussing this problem, with Elsie, she said that the word had circulated that I would ask them some questions about sexual matters. Elsie asked them, 'If you are ashamed to talk about these things with a doctor, why don't you hide your children?' It was an interesting rejoinder. On several occasions women who had freely admitted to me that they did not want any more children, at least not in the immediate future, would become completely unresponsive when I asked them what they knew about the various contraceptive measures available to them at the Mission hospital. Every explanation that I attempted to give in an educational way met with the same blank facial expression.

Elsie, too, found the lack of response of these women difficult to understand. The best explanation that she could offer involved the lack of verbal communication between a wife and her husband. 'Husbands and wives are too shy to speak, but keep on having babies. I keep telling them about the pill; it helped me a lot. They will not resist their husbands; maybe they fear that if they prevent having babies, their husbands might think they are being resisted. Others may be frightened to ask the nursing sister about it.'

It was Elsie's suggestion that an open discussion meeting concerning 'women's problems' be held for all those eighteen years old and over. This was announced at church, a day prior to the meeting. Eleven village women, ranging in age from eighteen to sixty-five, appeared, as well as the Missionary's wife and two nursing sisters.[3] Since there was a such a wide range in age, and to a certain extent in background (seven had lived in the dormitory at some time), and also because of their lack of experience with open discussions, the meeting at first moved very slowly. As the leader, I suggested several topics, including family matters. While all the women agreed that the man was the boss in the home, at least one admitted to verbal and physical fighting when there was a serious disagreement. I had hoped to get Elsie involved in a discussion about how to talk about sexual matters to her twelve-year-old daughter, but she was obviously unable to do so. In fact, all the mothers knew that their daughters learned about sex from older girls; but they were reluctant to take the initiative in such a discussion with their own children. This was not surprising considering their dormitory background.

When the older women, several of whom had given birth to eight or ten children, grasped the concept of voluntary limitation of family size, they thought it was a good idea. The younger women claimed they wanted only two children; several already had one or two, although unmarried. The group was asked whether in the old days there was any knowledge of how to induce abortion, but all denied this.

Another meeting was planned for the following week, but because of an outbreak of infectious hepatitis, it was not held. It was impossible to evaluate the impact, if any, of the single meeting. They had seemed enthusiastic about holding a second one, and several suggested that when Dr John Cawte came to the island, a comparable meeting should be held for the men and boys.

An outbreak of infectious hepatitis occurred in 1970, at the end of the dry season. The water supply in the wells was very low. With the occurrence of six cases of hepatitis within two days, all in children representing four families, it was decided that the school should close and that the majority of the people should evacuate the village and go to other parts of the island, or to neighbouring Denham Island, where the water supply was adequate. While this news took the villagers by surprise, they were not perturbed about it. In fact, some were delighted, since it was customary for many of them to take a holiday by 'going bush' just as soon as school closed for the December recess. Bush holidays allow the people to return to the life-styles of their ancestors.

Elsie's reactions to this epidemic, and to the idea of leaving the village, were interesting. She had had a glimpse at the children who were hospitalized and could see they were playing in their beds; so she did not think they were very sick. She was not concerned about the water shortage, either; she had experienced this before, and had drunk cloudy water most of her life. The thing that most impressed her was the flying-doctor's order to evacuate, as this had never happened before. She attempted to explain this order by saying, 'There are too many people now; so much sickness.'

Elsie thought of the old days, when there was not adequate shelter, and people just had to sit in the rain. The Roughsey family did not have either a moveable iron hut or a tent to make an adequate shelter if they left the village, and Elsie did not like the possibility of having to camp out in the rain. She disregarded the fact that she could easily have returned to her own house from the neighboring island if the rains came. Her husband wanted to go to the neighboring island, because they had been told to do so. After several days of musing about this, they remained in their own home in the village, along with about a dozen other families. I inferred that the main reason Elsie did not want to leave the village was that she feared our meetings would be interrupted, although I had assured her I would arrange transportation so that we could continue to meet.

Elsie always showed interest in any activities on the island: 'The possibility for jobs is so limited. It's a dull life here, no movies, no sports. The people are tired and weary. A lot of things we need, but we don't know how to go about getting them. There is nothing here like in the outside world. But we are having cricket now. There should be some activity or pleasure for everyone. The work up at Birri is brightening our lives. Maybe we can get more going in handcraft.'

Elsie had many ideas for activities ranging from sports for the village, church socials, to various types of outings. However, there was often a hiatus between the initiation of an idea and the formulation of plans to execute it. This inability to carry out an idea was not only a characteristic of Elsie, but of most of the Islanders.

For example, when Elsie and several of the other women had suggested that we should have a fishing trip to neighbouring Denham Island several days hence, I had said that I would bring the food, and they were to make the other arrangements. When the time came to depart, none had made firm plans regarding which man would take us over to Denham in his dinghy. After some confusion we finally got to the other side of the channel. Only one woman had a fish hook of the size necessary to catch the fish that we hoped to get, and none had brought any bait! Perhaps this was a planned oversight. In any event, it was hinted that I should ask the white people who were running the prawn-freezing operation on Denham Island for some of their prawn for bait, which I did. The few fish that were caught were immediately cooked over an open fire and eaten by the women who had caught them. No one offered to share her catch with those of us who were not successful in our fishing.

In the intervening years since my first visit in 1970, Elsie had continued to be active and interested in local activities. When the school teacher who had been the church choir leader left the island, no one else would take this job; so Elsie did. I saw her direct the choir, which she did in a professional manner.

Several men who were artists flew in one day to discuss art classes for the school children. Elsie was all for this. In fact, she was interested in almost anything that promised to broaden the opportunities for the island people. Unfortunately, most showed very little response, which led Elsie to express the feeling that many of the people did not like her. She could not understand this nor be very specific about it.

When I later inquired about Elsie's feelings of rejection when talking with an informant-friend of Elsie's, she replied, 'There are a lot of grudges caused by jealousy, like when someone gets something better than the other person. Many people are jealous of Dick because he is known for his art. To spite him, they don't attend meetings he might call. Elsie may be disliked because she is not afraid to speak up and say what is on her mind. She is a Lardil and has standing among her people. Some of the mainlanders are jealous of her for that.'

Elsie had definite ideas concerning the political climate on the island. She disagreed with the opinion of the majority of the people about where the new school and hospital should be built. The vote had been for these to be constructed in the very sandy area near the Mission. Elsie felt these structures should be built on the ridge where the terrain is solid. To support this she, perhaps unknowingly, revealed her biblical training by saying, 'Build your house on a firm foundation;

don't be foolish and build it on sand.'

This topic led to a discussion of the imminent incorporation of the village, with the Aboriginal Board of Directors being responsible for management of all the activities. Elsie, like the vast majority of the Islanders, was very concerned about this. The reasons for concern varied from person to person, but most were quite worried.

Elsie's anxiety about the withdrawal of the Mission primarily centered about her feeling that the Mornington Island people were not ready for this type of responsibility. She thought that they did not know how to conduct business affairs, including such practical considerations as knowing how to order supplies, to run the wireless, or to keep track of financial accounts. In addition, she expressed the opinion that the young adults who were supposed to constitute the Board of Directors would be especially inept; it would be better to have the older ones (like her husband) on the Board.

Elsie's Attitude Towards White Australians

In addition to her life-long association with the Mission staff, Elsie, through her husband, had had moderate contact with urban Australians. She and Dick, with their children, had lived several times, for periods up to six months, in the vicinity of Cairns, a town of 20 000 with a predominantly white population. Their sojourn there was prompted by Dick's art work and his white associates. She thought that they did well in adjusting to living in this community because they were under the watchful eye of a close friend who was white: 'He looked over us; he had full control'.

Elsie reported some of her reactions to living in this town: 'The first time I was in Cairns was four years ago. I was excited, happy, I could see how big the place was. We all did various sorts of crafts; that is how we kept going in money. Our white friend kept us away from the other Aborigines, in case we got mixed up. We had a shower, a bathroom. I'd liked to go into the town to see all the people. It was exciting to see how they dressed and spent money. But I'd get so tired waiting for the bus to go back home; and I'd feel shy about having all those heavy bundles of food to carry.' She claimed that the last time they lived there, it was the children who wanted to come back home to the island. She implied that the older boys would go into town, get 'shot' with drink, dance and get into difficulty with the police; for that reason they came back to the island. When she returned she had missed 'T.V., fish and chips, and fresh foods'. Elsie thought that she would like to live more or less permanently in Cairns and to come to the island for holidays.

In 1970, while discussing the interaction of white people and Aborigines of Mornington, Elsie expressed the opinion that 'Aborigines need the guidance and teaching of white people'. She had in mind the need for direction in a wide range of activities, from planning special programmes at church to the learning of carpentry. She continued, 'Dick gets enthusiastic about ideas for developing craft industries, such as weaving and pottery making, on the island, but I think they would only be successful if they were under the close direction of white people. I'm amazed when I see the fruits and vegetables growing at Birri, on the other side of the island, since the irrigation system was developed by that white man. If he leaves the island like he says he will, I'm afraid it will all dry up.'[4]

Elsie expressed her positive feelings for the Missionary by saying, 'Mr Belcher has always looked after us to see that the island is not taken away by outside people. He understands our customs in a friendly and Christian way. He's a lovable person to us people when we are in trouble. When he goes on furlough, we are sad, flat; when he is here, we are really safe. He's a real protector for us.'

When asked if there is much anger towards the white man among the villagers, she said that 'if a white man tells a workman something, he may not like it. Sometimes he talks directly back to the white man, but I think he is still afraid to get angry at him. They talk among themselves. In a public meeting, they won't speak up if a white man is there, but say a lot if none is present. Dick and I try to explain what white man's life is like. They think it is too hard to live like white man and would rather live a simple life like they are living now.'

Elsie went on to say that the Missionary had a paper from the Government or Mission Board — she was not sure which — asking them if they would like to live as 'free people'. By this she understood that they would be expected 'to pay for everything. They fear they would not have enough money to get a home, and pay taxes. They think it a bit hard: they are not ready yet. They do not understand what it is like out among white citizens. It frightens them, because it means husband, wife, and boys all work to keep the home up.'[5]

While I felt that Elsie bore resentment, probably unconscious, toward white people and those whose standard of living was more comfortable, she did not express it. However, in a letter to me some six months later, Elsie wrote, 'you are one of the best white friends that I ever had. We were like sisters'. But several sentences later, when talking about a project to teach the school children some of the Aboriginal legends, she wrote, 'We will teach the things they don't know, of how things were done in our early days, before the white man came to take away all our good laws and customs, and put in their poor stuff.' At least, through the less personal medium of a letter, Elsie could reveal her ambivalence.

Anticipating a Trip to Sydney

When I returned to Mornington Island in 1973, immediately after telling me I was to stay at her house, Elsie announced that she and Dick were going to Sydney. They were to leave in four days in order to attend the official opening of the Opera House, at the time the Lardil corroboree dancers were to perform for the Queen. Understandably, Elsie was anticipating this trip with pleasure.

However, to my Western way of thinking she seemed to be making no plans for departure, such as thinking about what clothing she would take, or arranging for someone to look after and feed her younger children. No doubt she expected her kinship group to take this responsibility. I also had the impression that she half expected to be disappointed by not being able to make the trip; as if she had been disappointed too many times previously.

It was ironic that the day prior to the departure date, it was not clear whether the agency that was to supply the plane ticket had done so. She showed her disappointment by becoming peevish and declaring that she was not going.

The day for departure arrived. The ticket matter was clarified by the

Elsie and Dick leaving for Sydney in 1973

Mission Manager; one had been available for some weeks. Elsie quickly put a few personal articles into a plastic tote bag. A minor crisis arose when she had no shoes to wear. The dog had eaten them! The village clothing store unfortunately did not open on that day. Dick borrowed a pair of white sandals from a neighbour, but they were too large for Elsie's feet. It looked as if she were going to have to wear the over-sized sandals. The crisis was resolved when Elsie, while awaiting the plane's arrival, noticed a woman wearing tennis shoes and ankle socks. She asked to try them on for size. The fitted perfectly. Thus Elsie departed, with Dick, for Sydney.

Elsie's Intellectual and Emotional Relation to Me as a Friend

Elsie's ease in relating to Westerners, as well as her interest in things inside and outside herself, contributed to her selection as the subject of this life-history. Her desire to learn more about herself and others was expressed in a letter to me, written some weeks after my first departure: 'I have learnt so much from our talks. Thanks for the many wonders of life that I now know through the questions you asked. With the answers I gave you, it has been such a help for understanding about myself and human life.'

When I returned in 1973, we spontaneously embraced and she said, 'Virginia, you are my friend, you are going to stay with me.'

It was evident that the Roughseys had had to make some temporary arrangements to house two additional people. There were already seven people living in the new house, plus several nephews who would wander in to sleep. It was necessary for Elsie to borrow such things as extra bedcloths, dishes, cutlery and the like. However, this was not the first occasion for them to have white guests; several months previously another woman had spent some days with them.

The most important thing to Elsie was to spend as much time as possible with me, going over the manuscript and filling in additional material. Both she and I felt some urgency about being able to talk for long periods of time together, because of her proposed trip to Sydney. For this reason, we spent most of the time sitting on her front verandah. Elsie assumed her customary position of reclining on the floor, propped up by a pillow, while I, in typical Western style, sat on a chair.

Elsie's interest and involvement in hearing and understanding every word that I had written was pronounced. Whenever there was a passage that she did not quite understand, she would have me re-read, and then often she would enlarge and add additional information. If I expressed fatigue and suggested a break, Elsie would insist we continue the work. During the first day or so, if someone stopped by to yarn, she would quickly suggest that we were busy.

It was during these days that I repeatedly discussed with her and Dick my feeling that I would not want to publish any material that they might object to having made public. They were adamant that they wished their real names to be used, and that this disclosure was acceptable to them.

I think it is pertinent to repeat the reasons Elsie gave for wishing the material to be published without any distortion. 'I have nothing to be ashamed of, and you have written the material as I have known my life and lived it. I want the world to know what life is like here on Mornington Island. If any student can learn anything from the material, I will be happy.'

At this point she told of having talked to students at a college in Canberra, and mentioned how pleased she was to tell them about her life. When I eventually felt satisfied that in no way would I be violating any personal and confidential material concerning the Roughseys, I suggested to Elsie that she might like to be named as collaborator. This was immediately accepted by her, with obvious delight.

She further supported her interest in wanting people to study Aboriginal life by relating that she had spoken up at the meeting held in Canberra where a large number of Aborigines from various parts of Australia had gathered for a conference. A number from the Northern Territory were protesting the digging of graves by some anthropologists. She had told them that this was inappropriate, in that previously they had never paid any attention to the graves. She had reminded them that the people in the graves had been dead and buried long before the protestors had been born. She stated that it was important to Aborigines that people who studied them get as much information as possible.

Then she turned to speak of 'cheeky black urbans. They were talking so smart. They knew nothing or cared nothing for their own cultural customs, but now they are making a big fuss. They want to take over without having a white man as advisor. I told them there was no reason to put white man aside.'

When it became evident to Elsie (and me) that we were going to have time to finish the manuscript work, she became receptive to having others spontaneously join us on the porch. This was especially true during the evening hours. Most that came were relatives; her brother, brother-in-law and sister-in-law, the wife of her brother who was currently living with another, or unrelated neighbours. Sometimes they brought small children who played inside and eventually dropped off to sleep on the floor. The conversation flowed freely; none seemed inhibited by having Nancy and me present. Dick Roughsey, a gifted story teller, easily amused the group with some of his tales.

Stimulated by the presence of two Americans, there was reminiscing about events that occurred during World War II. Several American planes had crashed in the vicinity of the island, and some of the crews had been rescued. Elsie's brother was the runner between the village and the Australian army camp nearby.

When the time arrived for Elsie to leave for Sydney, we both expressed our mixed feelings; gladness that she could make the trip, and sadness that we might not meet again. Before boarding the plane she gave me a gift, an Aboriginal message stick,[6] with the carving of her totem, 'rough seas', on it. Needless to say, I was very appreciative and touched by this appropriate and thoughtful gift from Elsie Roughsey; one that I will certainly always treasure.

But this was not the last time that Elsie and I were to meet. Her plans about where she would stay in Sydney and how long she would remain had been indefinite. When I returned to Sydney ten days later, after a series of phone calls I was able to locate where she was staying. I sent a message to her that I would come to see her at a specific time, just the day prior to my return to the United States.

When I arrived at the migrant hostel, an attractive place somewhat like a college dormitory, I found a quiet and dejected Elsie. I could not really ascertain all of the elements that might account for her depression. She had sought medical treatment for her back and was receiving daily physiotherapy, which she did not feel was improving her condition. She was not sure of the diagnosis.[7] She found the trips to a downtown Sydney clinic a chore. She had little to say about the Opera House opening. The Lardil dancers, along with several others from Mornington, were staying at the same hostel.

Perhaps what was contributing to Elsie's depression was her awareness that probably this might be the last time we would ever meet, and she was experiencing sorrow, which she could not express. I certainly felt some and expressed it. Another factor, and possibly a more potent one, was that I was accompanied by a young Australian friend. We had just come from a luncheon and I was wearing a silk suit, a type of clothing she had never seen me wear. I had the distinct feeling that she had become acutely aware of the vast differences between our ways of life.

Later, in a letter to Elsie, I inquired about the feelings she had been experiencing when we had met in Sydney. This was her reply: 'I was very happy to see you, dear mate. I watched anxiously for you. Then you came. Those few happy moments were so exciting in my heart. You just don't know how bad I felt to say goodbye to you. I didn't want to show it to you to make you feel upset, but you are a wonderful friend. I will never forget you, pal. I will always write to you to show our friendship will always be true, no matter where you and I are. We will hear from each other whenever there are some sweet moments. I hope the book will come out to be a real helpful one and many other people will benefit from it. I'll do anything you ask me to do. You are my friend. Cherrio, my pal. God bless you.'

Notes

1. This was verified by others. She used to be rather difficult and would get into altercations with family members and others.
2. Elsie's example was in contradiction to the fact that ice cream was not available on the island.
3. It has been suggested that the presence of the Missionary's wife may have inhibited the discussion. This I doubt, as Mrs Belcher, an open and broad-minded person, appeared to have an easy and comfortable relationship with the village women. I felt Mrs Belcher to be helpful to me, as she was more familiar to the women than I.
4. Indeed, the irrigation project became inoperative when the white developer left. In 1973, a fishing camp was located at Birri; the area was leased by a group of Mt Isa men who would fly in for several days of fishing.
5. This was the initial move of the Mission in the development of the plan to turn the administration of the island over to the people, which was to result in the incorporation and the withdrawal of Mission supervision.
6. Message Stick: In the old days, although there was no written language, messages were sent to other camps on sticks bearing carved symbols. The one Elsie gave me was made from a piece of dark wood, about 40 centimetres long, 2.5 centimetres wide, about 0.6 centimetre thick, and tapered at the edges and ends. Both flat sides had irregular carvings, indicating waves of the sea (rough sea). Both ends of the stick had been decorated with cockatoo feathers.
7. Information received from the medical records of the Sydney Hospital Orthopaedic Outpatient Department revealed tenderness over the lumbo-sacral region on examination. An x-ray showed osteophyte lipping of L4, L5. She was ordered to have shortwave therapy and strengthening exercises.

10
The Other Women

Who were the other women on the island? What were they like? What did they have to say about themselves and their families? What were their ideals, goals, and frustrations? How were they different from, or how were they like Elsie? What did they think of each other? How did they interact? What traditional beliefs did they maintain? What did they think about the future?

Illustrative vignettes will be presented in an attempt to round out the picture of the women who now call Mornington Island home. They will be presented in three groupings: those considered Lardil, over thirty years of age, who were products of the Mission dormitory system; those Lardil under thirty, most of whom were raised on the island by their parents in a family situation; and those belonging to the Kaiadilt tribe, who were evacuated to the island in 1948. Approximately twenty women were interviewed from two to six hours each.

For various reasons several of the women were not on the island when I returned in 1973, so that the material could not be read to them. The life circumstance of each woman three years later will be mentioned.

The Women from the Dormitory Era
With the development of the dormitories for boys and girls, the Lardil who lived according to their traditional tribal customs apparently voluntarily permitted their children to be brought up separately from them at the Mission. As a result, from early childhood, there was only casual contact with the tribal relatives. The Missionary and his wife took over the parental roles. Consequently, most of the early memories of these middle-aged women were predominantly of the regimented dormitory life.

Also in this group were the women who had been born on the mainland, frequently the offspring of European-Aboriginal sexual unions. The Aboriginal parent (or parents) usually belonged to one of the tribes in the coastal area adjacent to the southern part of the Gulf of Carpentaria. My informants' memories of their parents, or of life prior to their being sent to the Mission, were largely dependent on their age upon arrival. Since they had spent all or part of their youth with the Lardil girls, and had married young men who were members of the comparable boys group, they were primarily both socially and culturally identified with the indigenous Lardil group. However, when interpersonal difficulties have occurred, it was still remembered that they were not really Lardil.

Let us discover what these other middle-aged women had to say.

Hannah Nelson: aged forty-two

'It's going to be awful if the Mission leaves.'

Hannah was concerned about her children, seven in number, ranging in age from six to twenty. She wanted her children to have a better life than she had known. 'When they finish school, I'd like them to train for something, but the boys are so lazy. They won't carry water or chop wood, or even light the fire. I do all the growling, as my husband is on their side. It makes it hard for the mothers. I see the same in my neighbours. My husband won't chop wood either. When he's sick, I have to be mother and wife to him. He just sits. I feel I'm being punished instead of Adam. I think I will have the doctor look at my husband's brains as well as his body.'

When I arrived at Hannah's house, both she and her husband were looking at books containing pictures. I inquired about them. They were books of Bible stories that one of their sons had received for perfect attendance at Sunday school. Her husband often told the children Biblical stories. Hannah hoped that at least one son would be a minister or at least would study the Bible.

Hannah related that years ago an uncle had been speared by one of the Bentinck Island people. His boat was smashed and burned, and he was killed. I wondered how she had felt about the Bentinck people when they had been brought to Mornington Island. To this she replied, 'All was forgiven, "for they know not what they do". They must have had a bad chief like the story of Nebuchadnezzar in the Bible; he was a bad leader.'

Several years previously Hannah had been sent to the mainland to be delivered of a stillborn baby; her health was very bad. 'The doctor told me he could put something in me to prevent more babies. I took it as doctor's orders; he knew best. I could have had another baby after the dead one, but I felt like refusing another pregnancy after being so sick. I heard some of the women say doctors could put something in you, and I thought one day the doctor would say that would be for me.' She would never have thought of asking for birth control, but when she heard it as an order, then it was welcomed. There seemed to be some guilt connected with the idea of preventing pregnancy.

Hannah said she would not consider telling other women that she was using a birth control device, 'because they might throw it up if there would be an argument.[1] They think it funny or rude to talk about the body. They think pulling down clothes in front of a doctor is a shameful thing, but they pull down their pants in the bush with men.' These attitudes might explain in part the resistance of some of the younger women to talk about birth control.

Both of Hannah's elder children were girls who were working in a hospital on the mainland. She had told them both that they 'must live in the right way until they marry; it's good to be with your husband, not otherwise'. She also told them not to go with a white man, because she did not want 'a grandchild that might not want to know me because I have dark skin'.

Hannah had aspirations for her children with respect to both an education and a moral, productive life. It remained to be seen whether her unmarried daughters would be able to remain virtuous, as their mother wished, and whether her sons would exert the energy or discipline needed to be other than unskilled labourers. She did not feel that her husband represented a strong model for their sons to pattern after.

When I saw Hannah three years later, she was most preoccupied by a recent fight in the village. 'I was in the hospital for several days. My blood pressure was up and I was having headaches, so the sisters thought I should have a rest. But then that terrible fight broke out. The canteen was open in the morning and again later. I don't think beer should be allowed. Then some young blokes drank some spirits. I don't know where they got it. Several started making nasty remarks to some girls who also were drinking. One girl's brother started to hit the others with a boomerang; then everything went wild.

'I could hear it in the hospital. The police brought several bloody ones to the hospital. They used terrible language to the sisters, who were trying to stop the bleeding. I couldn't stand it, so I asked a policeman to walk me home. I couldn't hear or see what was going on from my house.

'I heard that the sisters had to spend the whole night sewing up the cuts. Some even had to stay in the hospital, they were so bad off. I don't know what I would have done if I had been too sick to leave. I probably would have had a heart attack; I did have some chest pain.

'It's going to be awful if the Mission leaves. I wonder if the teachers and sisters will stay. I'm afraid we are going to kill each other. We have always had fights, but this drinking will be the end of us.'

Pearl Yates: aged fifty-eight

'If you don't respect your children, they won't respect you.'

These words were spoken by the mother of ten children, five boys and five girls, ranging in age from 16 to 34. All but the two youngest sons and a married daughter were living away from the island and had jobs, some of a skilled nature.

Pearl was half-European; she had been sent from the mainland to the Mission dormitory at the age of eight. She had lived there until her marriage to a dormitory-reared Lardil, who courted her for several years. She was tall, thin, with high cheek bones. Her poise and easy-going manner inspired confidence. She was a quiet, unassuming leader. Both she and her husband had worked constantly at various Mission jobs throughout their married life. Because of his age, her husband was receiving old-age pension fortnightly. During the alternate week, they sold handcrafts, so that money was available for their needs.

Pearl had some vivid memories of the events surrounding her becoming a dormitory resident. In fact, her story brings to mind the word 'kidnapped'. Her father, a white man, and her mother, an Aborigine, worked on a cattle station on the mainland. Her father also carried mail from Riversleigh to Burketown by buggy. She had two brothers and a sister. Her mother took an orphaned Aboriginal girl baby into their home. The station manager thought it best for this child to be sent to the Mornington Island Mission. Pearl's grandmother drove the orphan to Burketown, and Pearl went along for the ride. However, the Burketown police persuaded the grandmother to send Pearl to the Mission also. Pearl now supposes that her grandmother was helpless in the situation.

Pearl remembered crying and crying for a long time after being put into the dormitory. When she learned to write, the letters sent to her parents would be read to them by the station manager so that contact, although minimal, was maintained. Some thirty years later, the manager's grand-daughter came to Mornington as a teacher and made herself acquainted with Pearl. It was in 1967, some forty-seven years later, that Pearl visited her old mother on the mainland. At this point she became slightly tearful and said, 'It was sad not to have lived with my mother during childhood, but I was glad to have seen her again, if only one time.' Her father had died some years previously.

It was of interest to learn what Pearl's grown children were doing.

Two sons were welders in Brisbane; both were unmarried and lived with a white family. Another son, married, with two children, worked on the roads in Cloncurry. Three of her daughters were married to men holding jobs in various Queensland towns: one son-in-law worked in a post office, one worked in the Mt Isa mines, and another as a car mechanic. An unmarried daughter was a domestic. Three of Pearl's children continued to live on the island. A daughter, married, with six children, worked as a nurse's aide; a married son was a mechanic, and a single son was a stockman. She did not mention whether or not all of her children were married to Aborigines.

I remarked that all her children were doing relatively well in contrast to those of many other women, and asked her how she accounted for this. She replied, 'I always gave them jobs to do. I would talk to them and punish them if they didn't do something. Many mothers say they can't boss their children. These mothers never speak in a quiet, sensible way, but yell and swear. If you speak in a nice clean way, children will notice.' Then she made the remarkable statement, 'If you don't respect your children, they won't respect you.' While she considered her husband to be a quiet man, she always had talked things over with him. She said that if she had a burden he would always come to help. 'We have always been keen workers, and the children know this.'

Pearl spoke more of her child-rearing practices. She had breast-fed her children until they were about age one. Prior to weaning, she gave them other foods, such as porridge, soup, and milk. She had experienced difficulty in weaning only one child; and she did this by putting chilli powder on her nipples. In retrospect, she thought that the children had been about six to seven months old when she began bowel training. She kept a tin can by their bed, and put them on it in the middle of the night. If they messed, she would 'growl' at them and show them the tin. She was also teaching her grandchildren who were on the island in the same way when they became toddlers. She then made the statements, 'If they learn to be tidy when they are young, they will be tidy when they grow up.'[2]

Since Pearl had been born on the mainland and had never been 'adopted'[3] by any Lardil family, she had no 'kin' of her own. While she acknowledged the importance of kinship groupings among the Islanders, she denied that she had missed this since becoming an adult. She claimed that she had felt like a member of her husband's kin group. In contrast to when she was young, she no longer minded the absence of a father-uncle on whom to depend.

She admitted that there could be nasty gossip among many of the women. Some have accused the former mainland women, whose children tended to hold better jobs, both on and off the island, of 'pushing' their children and of getting preferential treatment for them. At such times, the indigenous women might make a nasty remark: 'You think you are something 'cause you're half-white, or, you're from the mainland.' When Pearl, who certainly could not be described as arrogant in any way, had been thus accused, she had felt that she must argue back; otherwise they would have continued to accuse her.

She was somewhat reluctant to talk about sorcery. She had heard about it, but did not know whether to believe in it or not. 'I'm not sure if some deaths are a result of this or are natural deaths from God's will. I believe that our lives are kept in God's hand. I don't know if God would work through a sorcerer or not.' It had never occurred to her to discuss this with the Missionary. She had had to develop her own rationalization to explain these two disparate beliefs. She claimed that she had never feared that she would be a victim.

She was equally unsure about the phenomenon of *malgri*. Pearl said, 'It's hard to know. About five years ago, when my one son was about twelve, he went swimming after eating tinned meat. Later he said he had to do 'pooey', but couldn't, and had a lot of pain. I took him to the nursing sister, who give him enemas and medicine. It went on for four days; it was no good, no poocy. So, I then took him to the old Songman, who started to rub, sing, and blow, and then said, "you will be all right". Later, he had to go to the pot and really relieved himself of the mess. So, I don't know if I believe in *malgri* or not.'

Previously, Pearl had not heard, or at least had not let it register on her consciousness, that there are various methods of birth control. This emerged when the subject was discussed at the open meeting for the women. At that time she had nineteen grandchildren; and when it was suggested that the older women could pass this information on to their daughters and daughters-in-law, she expressed great reluctance for fear that they would regard this as meddling in their lives. This fear of expressing ideas or opinions was not unique to Pearl. Among her age group there was marked inclination to avoid being 'bossy' or causing dissension.

Three years later, Pearl no longer was living in a mud-floor house in the old part of the village. She and her husband had moved to one of the new houses several months prior to my second visit to the island. The move was suggested by one of her daughters. Although she and her husband had worked many years for the Mission and were certainly eligible for a new house, they felt that parents with small children should have them. They made application only after making very sure no other family wanted the house at that time.

Another factor which contributed to the Yates's decision to move to a new house was the feeling that their seven children who lived on the mainland might not like a 'dirt house' when they came back for visits. However, Pearl felt that they had never acted strangely when they visited, but seemed to fit into Mornington life quite easily. They simply took off their city clothes and shoes and became island people again.

On the mainland, Pearl's children were living in predominantly white communities. She had visited them, and thought it was good to 'live in a clean way'. I asked what had impressed her most when she visited Brisbane. She had some difficulty putting this into words. About all she could say was, 'People dress differently; they wear shoes all the time.'

The Yates's new home was kept very clean. In the kitchen all the food was in canisters and there was no evidence of roaches or other bugs. The furnishings included a second-hand electric refrigerator, a table, a number of chairs, several beds and chests. Pearl said she had never been comfortable sitting on chairs until she had moved to the new house. She liked the new home because it was easier to keep clean and tidy; one could move about more freely, and get better rest (in contrast to the cramped area in the mud-floor house).

When I told her that I wished to read to her the material I had previously written, and the reasons why, Pearl initially looked a little startled, but said she would like to hear it. She was obviously pleased, and said that everything was satisfactory, including the use of a pseudonym.

Catherine Elong; aged thirty-eight
'How could I go about getting a divorce?'

Catherine was tall, with medium brown skin, straight black braided hair, and high cheek bones over slightly sunken cheeks; she was half-European. I had seen her preside over a women's group at church, and while she did not express herself in any notable way, she appeared to have more command of herself and the situation than most local women.

When I appeared for the interview, she was filling a very large rusty barrel with water from a large tank. She quickly explained that the water was clean, but the tank was rusty, and that they did not drink the water. We then went to sit on a porch-like arrangement of her one-room corrugated leanto in which she had been living since separating, five months previously, from her husband of eighteen years.

She began her story by saying, 'My mother brought me and my five brothers and sisters to the Mission when I was three years old. I began living in the dormitory when I was five. The dorm was good, but not a happy place. We never had the opportunity to see anything, but it did keep control over young people.' She remained there until she married. As she told the story, one day the Missionary asked her if she would mind marrying Vernon, and she replied that she would; so the wedding took place in less than a week. Her husband, Vernon, who was half-Chinese, had been raised in the boy's dormitory.

Catherine continued by saying, 'I married him to get my freedom from the dormitory. The marriage was never any good. It was with someone I never loved. I don't hate him, or even dislike him; it was just an empty feeling all the time. That's why I am now living in this shack. I left him, or he drove me out of the house. I didn't ever feel love; it makes me sad to think of it. The marriage was wrong from the beginning; he was always suspicious and accusing. I feel happier since I left my husband; satisfied and safe. I have never thought of going back.'

It was at this point that she asked me how she might go about getting a divorce. I told her I was not familiar with divorce laws in the State of Queensland but that perhaps she could seek advice and information through the Mission office. She then went on to say that she thought her husband would agree to a divorce since they both had felt better since they had separated.

I then confronted her with the fact that I knew that she had a one-year-old child, fathered by Norman, another man in the village. To this she replied yes, and said that according to Norman their relationship was a part of 'dark people's customs'.[4] She went on to explain that 'something special' happened between her and the other man, and that this 'something special' was not meant for her husband, Vernon. This seemed to help her rationalize the event. She added, 'There is no trouble in my mind, just in other people's. There was a fuss for a little while, then everything calmed down.'

This woman had always been a respected member of the community, and had worked as a teacher's assistant for many years. Her two older children were off the island, one working, the other in boarding school. She had hopes that her children would have a better chance in life than she had had. After expressing these hopes, she requested that I talk with her daughter, Ida, when she returned for the Christmas holidays. Ida had just written that she was unhappy and did not want to remain in the boarding school.

The preceding material was written about Catherine at the time of my first trip to the island. I learned to know her much better during my second trip. She seemed particularly friendly when she met me at the air-strip, and during the days that I was living with the Roughseys. She, as did many others, stopped by several times for a long yarn. She, like Elsie, was very comfortable in making conversation with Nancy Waxler and me. This was Dr Waxler's first contact with Aborigines, although she had spent extensive periods in other isolated parts of the world. She was repeatedly surprised how open people like Elsie, Catherine, and others were in expressing Western ideas, as well as in freely discussing their tribal beliefs.

Various subjects would occur either spontaneously or as a result of Nancy's and my questions. The ideas that emerged in our discussions certainly had a strong Western flavour. It is, of course, not entirely possible to determine how strongly our presence influenced their responses. In discussing the education of the island children, especially the brighter ones, Catherine expressed the opinion that children should be sent away to boarding school when they were about age ten rather than waiting until they were sixteen, as then they were so far behind their own age group that they were bound to feel inferior. She then told us about a recent teachers meeting she had attended in a distant city; and expressed the opinion that, if she were a trained teacher looking for a job on the mainland, there would be no discrimination because of her race.

We talked of a recent newspaper article which had reported that an Aboriginal girl in the Northern Territory had been given to a white couple by the parents as an infant. Now, some eight years later, upon the demand of the Aboriginal tribe, the child was being returned to her natural parents, much against the white couple's wishes. They had considered her their own adopted child. Both Elsie and Catherine thought that she should be allowed to remain with the adoptive parents, as no doubt the child regarded them as her mother and father and was a stranger to her tribal family. This led into a story of Catherine's in which she related how a white woman had wanted to take a child of hers, but not until he was six years old. Catherine said that it might be possible for a mother to give a child up for adoption at the time of his birth, but never after she had learned to know and love him.

When I talked with Catherine individually, she preferred to meet me in the Mission area. I explained to her that I wished her approval for what I had written about her and her daughter (Ida Elong) after my first visit to Mornington. She readily accepted what I had recorded and then went on to give me much additional information.

She said that Norman, her lover, had come back to live with her permanently soon after I left the island three years previously (a fact which I had already learned, as there are hardly any secrets in this small closed community). She said that at that time there had been a big fight between her legal husband's family,[5] who came from the mainland, and Norman.

I had already heard that Norman had recently beaten her badly, and that his relatives had had to come to her rescue. About this episode, Catherine said, 'He only fights and accuses me when he is drunk. I feel the hurt for a while but I get over it. Everything is satisfactory between us when he is not drinking.'[6]

During this conversation, we got into her beliefs about *puri-puri* (sorcery). I found her to be intense on the subject. She gave the impression that her involvement with *puri-puri* had been at least accentuated by her association with Norman, who seemed to be relinquishing the Mission influences. She thought that both Norman and her legal spouse, Vernon, worried most of the time that one would put *puri-puri* on the other. Death results from *puri-puri*.

Catherine said she had never known how *puri-puri* was done, but she had seen people suffer and die from it. She then launched into a long story about a nine-year-old boy who had died four months previously. 'He was a healthy, happy child, interested in learning. Suddenly he became ill; his whole body was swollen. He was treated by the sisters until the flying-doctor sent him to the Brisbane Hospital, but they couldn't cure him. He died a few days after being sent back here.' She went on to say that the boy's father thought that someone with whom he had had a fight meant to put *puri-puri* on him, but the son caught the evil spell by mistake. This could have happened if the boy had touched something that the father was meant to touch. Catherine thought that perhaps one day the father would get back at the sorcerer by having someone do it to him.[7]

Catherine went on to give other information about the concept of *puri-puri*. A sorcerer might take an item of clothing from his victim, say a shirt, and cut off a sleeve. Then he would hide the shirt in a hollow log. Eventually the victim would develop a sore on his arm where the sleeve had been cut and no one could cure the sore. Catherine, as did a number of others, said that the Lardil were particularly afraid of mainland Aborigines (she did not include herself as one) as potential sorcerers. Catherine had avoided going among mainland Aborigines for fear that she might become a victim.

When discussing the subject of totems, Catherine said, 'My totem is the dog. It's inherited like skin (headedness). If I dream of the dog, someone would say "that is your uncle or cousin from the Dreamtime. Maybe he is coming back home without your knowing it".' Recently, while she was away at the teachers' meeting, she dreamed of a snake. She knew 'there would be trouble when I got home, since a snake is the symbol of an enemy. It came true. The enemy was Norman. He beat me up after accusing me of being with other men.'

We also talked about 'madness'. Catherine thought that worry caused madness in Europeans, but that 'Aborigines feel their worries in their stomach. When I feel worried by things like people growling or throwing nasty hints at me, I go off some place and sit alone until the worry goes out of my stomach.' She thought that madness in Aborigines is caused by lack of sex.

In Catherine's comparison of European and Aboriginal responses to worry, she said that she was 'proud' to have chosen to be an Aborigine. She expressed the opinion that those who have 'passed' as white were sorry they had joined the European society and had forgotten all about their culture. I asked her about her daughter, Ida, who was only half Aborigine and whose boyfriend was probably only a quarter Aborigine. I commented that a child of this union might easily pass as white. Her reply was that it would be up to them whether or not they raised a child in the Aboriginal tradition, but that she would be sorry if they didn't.

In discussing the changes that had occurred on the island during her lifetime, she spoke of the better homes (she was then still in her 'shack'), improved education, better food supply, regular boats and aircraft coming in, better clothing and health care. When I asked about the non-material, more psychological changes she replied, 'There is less happiness, more trouble in the village. When we were children in the dormitory, we were protected from the outside trouble. Now children, as well as adults, see and feel the trouble. There is more general dissatisfaction. People used to be satisfied with what they had; they had to depend on themselves.' Catherine hoped that in years to come there would be more happiness when everyone would get the homes, education and health care they needed.

Lillie Tanner: aged fifty-one
'To be married to my husband is the most important thing.'

'Norman chose me to marry. He visited me on Sundays on the Mission verandah for three years, bringing me gifts such as fish and sugarbag. We went to the next island on a two-week honeymoon. It was a good honeymoon.' With this, Lillie smiled with a pleased, contented expression. She said this during my first visit to the island.

Prior to the interview, I had seen Lillie only in groups, where she spoke very little or not at all. However, during our private meeting she was amazingly open and verbal. Among other things, she went on to tell me that her health had always been satisfactory. Out of ten pregnancies, six children were still living. About two years earlier she had gone through the 'change of life'. She had had regular periods until one month she bled for one day only, and then no more. She had thought she was pregnant, and after three months she went to the nurse. She had felt sad when she was told she was not pregnant, but probably menopausal. She had felt sorry that she could not have any more children.

She continued by saying that the most important thing in her life was being married to her husband, Norman, and being with him all the time. At this point, because she seemed to be avoiding the village information, I gently introduced the subject of her husband's infidelity (it was he who had fathered Catherine Elong's child) by saying that she must have felt very troubled during the last several years. Her reply was, 'Things are all right between us now, but it was very hard for several years. I was hurt and had many bad thoughts about her. I kept all my feelings inside, but three times I did lose my temper when I saw her. I wanted to hit her, and even tried. I would read my Bible and say my prayers. When I'd have restless nights, I'd pray and then I could sleep. I never said anything to Norman. I was angry at her, not him. She was the one at fault; I blamed her for not driving him away, although he went to her. We had had such good years until 1968.'

Lillie claimed that she considered marital relations were mainly for pleasure and not a duty. She experienced satisfaction most of the time. 'I feel a good weakness afterwards. It was hard to accept him (sexually) when all that trouble was going on, but I have forgiven him. We now have relations about two times a week.'

Sexual promiscuity was said to be common on the island, especially among the younger people. However, similar behaviour, resulting in a pregnancy, on the part of those who were middle-aged and responsible members of the community would create a public scandal. The husband of the 'other woman', Catherine Elong, brought the matter up before the village Council, and Norman was ordered to contribute to the financial support of the child, and was forbidden to see Catherine. Thus, the scandal seemed to have been resolved, if not forgotten, by those involved, and by the villagers.

The remarkable aspect was the persistence of Lillie in placing all the responsibility on the 'other woman', and in not berating her husband at any time. Being able to displace all her anger to Catherine allowed Lillie to see her husband as blameless. She was reported to have said to a member of the Mission staff that her husband was 'perfect'. No doubt her over-evaluation of her husband all during their marriage allowed for this defensive maneouvre at a time of crisis.

However, in 1973, Lillie appeared sad and desolate. Norman was staying all the time with Catherine. Lillie said, 'At first he would go away at night and come back at day break. I never asked him where he was, but I had my ideas. I felt very angry inside at him and Catherine, but I wouldn't talk about it.

'Then, he didn't come back at all. When the children and I would be ready to eat, they would say "we are fatherless" and I would agree. But we would never say anything to him, not even the older boys. We were afraid he would fight us. I am sad and angry. I have so little money, Norman gives me so little. He doesn't work and makes few handcrafts. I get a little money from child endowment. Friends give me food. I guess he loves Catherine more than me. I don't know how *puri-puri* is done. If I did, I might try it.'

Lillie kept all her anger and sadness inside her, apparently without any secondary symptoms such as insomnia, weight loss or other physical difficulty. Several people mentioned to me that she seemed to be 'managing well'. They must have shut their eyes to her obvious sadness. One could only wonder how she contained her feelings. I certainly had no impression that she was enjoying her suffering. There appeared to be little or nothing that could be interpreted as emotional support.

Her distress was accentuated by the fact that her sister had left her two young sons with her when she went to the mainland, and had 'forgotten' to leave Lillie any money for their food. After expressing her dilemma to several people, the village Council met and decided that Lillie's grown sons should advance her money which would be charged against the sister's account. Lillie did manifest resentment at being put in this position by her sister. Her older sons did not voluntarily supply her with money to feed their cousins. Evidently kinship obligations and generosity had their limits.

When I introduced the subject of the people taking over the running of the island, Lillie replied, 'It will be very hard in every way. Now there is stealing, drinking, and gambling. People don't go to church. Maybe in three or five years we will learn. It will be better than now if the young people will take responsibility.'

Ethel Tunney: aged forty

'There is a time to love children and a time to be hard on them.'

I had noticed Ethel several times while passing her home, prior to my suggesting an interview. She appeared to be one of the most industrious and organized women on the island. When I had seen her, Ethel was always washing, cooking, or making shell pins and necklaces.

In 1970, her house contained conveniences which were unique to the island homes at that time. Spigots furnished running water for her laundry tubs, which in turn had drains to let out the used water. A kerosene 'fridge' provided refrigeration.

When I came for the interview, she was ready to tell me her story in her organized fashion and had chairs available for us to sit on. She apologized for having her eighteen-month-old son present, thinking he might distract our attention. She quickly launched into the story of her life.

Ethel was born on the island and was educated in the dormitory system. Both her mother and father, who were still alive, had always worked for the Mission so that she had seen them daily. She had never lost contact with her own parents, in contrast to many of the dormitory-reared children.

When she was eighteen, her father had wanted her to marry a man of her mother's people on the mainland to whom she had been promised according to kinship rules. To quote Ethel, 'I told him I would not marry a man that I didn't know, and he left it at that. Instead, I married Sam. We were in love. He was born here on Mornington, like me, but I hadn't been promised to him like I had been to the other bloke. I think the Missionary talked to our parents so that they didn't fuss when Sam and I said we were going to get married.

'My husband has always been so smart and hard working. You know he's the boss of the maintenance crew. He's a good man. He's a church elder and a member of the Council.

'He is still so good-looking. When we were first married, I was afraid other women might run after him because of his looks. He was tall and thin and neat, and I have always been short, sloppy, and fat.' Sam was always neatly dressed and groomed and had a dignified manner; Ethel was obese with bushy hair. Both had very dark skins, both having only Lardil ancestors.

Ethel continued, 'I finally decided that the jealousy was all in my head, no reason for it. Since I have stopped accusing him, we have gotten along fine. I like being Sam's wife.

'I've had eight babies, one died when he was born. My oldest boy, Ben, is on the mainland learning to repair motors. My seventeen-year-old girl, Martha, is going to business school. I hope she will come back here and work in the Mission office. All of our children do good in their studies and don't give us much trouble. My girl, Bertha, is tricky. I have to keep an eye on her.' When I asked her what she thought was the most important thing in raising children, Ethel replied, 'There is a time to love them, and a time to be hard on them.'

Just after making this remark, two of her younger children arrived home from school. The warm, but rather quiet manner in which they greeted their mother and baby brother seemed to reflect Ethel's child-rearing philosophy. Ethel appeared to have amalgamated the discipline of the dormitory and the acceptance (and no doubt love) of her own parents by becoming a loving mother with a firm approach.

When I returned to Mornington three years later, Ethel was eager to talk to me. The family continued to live in the same house. She had many things on her mind which she rapidly related: 'Sam's been in the hospital in Mt Isa for over a month. The flying-doctor sent him there to have his rupture fixed, but something went wrong. He's having trouble with his legs, something about his veins (phlebitis). He wrote me the

other day and said his legs are better, but he's worried if he can still
work as hard as he always has.

'Ben is working in a factory in Townsville. I think he's doing all
right, and Martha is back here working in the office like I hoped she
would. I think she'd like to get a job in Brisbane or Townsville where
there is more to do.

'The one I worry about is Bertha. I think we did right, but I don't
know. She's sixteen now, but last year she had a baby; she was hardly
fifteen. The bloke who got her in this family way had been sent here
'cause he was making trouble at another Mission. He only caused
trouble here, so the Mission sent him back to the mainland.

'Sam and I worried. We like our grandchild, but supposing that
Bertha liked another boy. I was sort of tired of having babies around
after my last one. The flying-doctor had put something in me to stop me
from having babies. After Bertha had her child, Sam and I went to the
Missionary and to the flying-doctor. After a lot of talk, we decided to go
ahead and have the same thing put in Bertha. I can't keep my eye on her
all the time. Do you think that was the right thing to do?'

After obtaining more details, especially about Bertha's feelings
concerning the pregnancy, the baby, and the contraceptive device, I
attempted to be reassuring about the decision she and her husband had
made. She appeared relieved.

Finally I was able to read to her the material I had recorded after our
talk three years earlier. Ethel's response was a mixture of pleasure and
embarrassment. She was obviously flattered. She then became quiet and
thoughtful, and finally spoke, 'Yes, my parents loved me, and the
Missionary and his wife showed me how to be firm. I guess I didn't go
wrong with Bertha. She was just young and finding out about things.'

Later, she told me that it was all right with her for me to write about
all that had happened to her and Sam and their children.

Nettie Long; aged sixty-seven
Nurri-Nurri: 'It feels so good to bleed.'

Nettie, although Christian, under certain circumstances reverted to
an ancient tribal expression of emotion by performing *nurri-nurri,* the
self-infliction of bodily wounds in order to demonstrate one's sorrow or
joy, traditionally only performed by women. Nettie declared that she
did *nurri-nurri* because, 'It feels so good to bleed.'

In performing *nurri-nurri,* knives, spears, shells, stones, bits of glass
or any sharp object at hand may be used. The last time Nettie had done
this was about a year previously when her eldest son returned home
after an absence of five years. She had met him at the airstrip. Over-
whelmed with 'joy', she had stabbed the top of her head with a knife so

that blood had poured over her face. Another son had intervened to prevent further injury. In recounting the event to me she explained, 'I was showing my oldest son how much I had missed him.'

Nettie had injured herself on several other occasions earlier in her life. She had cut herself upon the death of one of her children, and upon hearing of her mother's death. Nettie actually had not seen her mother for many years, as her mother was living on another Mission. As a result of repeated self-injuries, she had many scars on her legs and head.

A few other older Lardil women also had practised *nurri-nurri* in years past. However, the older Kaiadilt women have continued a similar custom to the present time. Elsie and most of the Lardil women said that it had never occurred to them to perform *nurri-nurri*. They implied that it was only those women who had not had the Christian influence of the dormitory who occasionally cut themselves when they experienced intense feelings.

Nancy Vines: aged fifty-five, and Ellen: aged eighteen
'She's not keen on boys.'

Nancy Vines, aged fifty-five, and her daughter Ellen, aged eighteen, attended the discussion meeting that I held for the women of the island. This type of shared interest seemed rather unusual. As it turned out, Ellen would go nowhere without her mother. Or, perhaps, Ellen was not allowed to go anywhere without her mother as chaperone.

Nancy was one of the half-caste waifs who had been brought to the Mission from the mainland to be raised in the dormitory. Her marriage of thirty-three years to a Lardil had been arranged by the Missionary. She had mothered six sons and Ellen. The three eldest sons worked away from the island, two had married, but as yet Mrs Vines had no grandchildren. She knew her children were industrious, but she worried that they might drink too much.

In 1970, the Vines's house was one of the largest on the island, consisting of four bedrooms, a kitchen, a bathroom, and a verandah. Nancy was grey-haired, dignified, and neat. In discussing her household, she mentioned that she wished there were some way to hang up her clothing after ironing, instead of folding and putting it in boxes. I showed her a metal rod in the makeshift clothes closet that I was using, and suggested that if she had no metal rod, a broom-handle would suffice to hold hangers, which were sold at the store. I ventured to suggest that one of her sons could help her install such a simple arrangement. She seemed surprised that a problem that had been concerning her could be so easily solved.

In talking about her daughter, Ellen, Nancy said, 'She is not keen on boys. She doesn't sit or talk with them. I urge her to go to dances with her brothers, but she wants me to come with her.'

Ellen's lighter skin reflected her partly white ancestry. She was painfully shy and had great difficulty in communicating with me. She was equally reserved with the teacher with whom she worked as an assistant, and talked only to the students. She had worked for a brief period at a cattle station, but wanted to come back to the island 'to her mum'. She had never gone with a boy, although she denied being afraid of them. She reported that her mother had warned her, 'Don't go with boys; boys get you pregnant.' At that point her eyes started filling with tears. I attempted to be as supportive as possible, but she could say little more on this or any subject. As nearly as I could ascertain, her fantasy life was as constricted as her social life. She could express no wishes for herself. Her mother hoped that her daughter would marry a good man, not a drunkard, and have a good home.

Evidently Nancy Vines had guarded and warned her daughter about the evils of men as zealously as had the Missionary's wife in her own time. How was it that the dormitory teachings had been passed on to this daughter, when there was little evidence of this type of morality in the offspring of most of the other dormitory-reared parents? Would Ellen only wed if the marriage were arranged for her in a manner similar to the practices of the dormitory days?

My speculation about the role of the chaperone was answered when I returned to the island. I chatted with Nancy Vines one day when she was sitting on the beach some distance from the village. She was watching her husband and several other men standing in the water over the reef, spearing fish with long poles to which three metal prongs were attached to gig the fish. Nancy had made a lean-to to protect her from the sun. She had a thermos bottle, a plastic bowl containing a loaf of unbaked damper, and several other containers. She was planning to cook the fish that her husband speared. It was a very pleasant picnic scene.

Among other things, we spoke of her children. Without any apparent hesitation, she told me that Ellen was staying at Mt Isa, waiting to have a baby (all women who were having their first child were then sent to Mt Isa for delivery). Nancy continued, 'She was always shy, but she went to the mainland for a holiday. After she returned, I thought she might be pregnant, but I said nothing to her. I talked to one of the nursing sisters, who had the same idea; so I told Ellen to go to see the sister. Our suspicions were right.'

As far as I was able to determine there had been no conversation between Nancy and her daughter concerning the pregnancy. It was treated as an unspoken fact. When her mother abstained from her role as chaperone, Ellen became pregnant. However, I did not detect any evidence of hurt or malice about the fact in the mother's attitude.

Ginny Cole: aged thirty-nine

'Are you going to write a book?'

Ginny began the interview by asking if a book were going to be written as a result of my investigation, and if real names would be used. She was told that if anything were published, fictitious names would be used; and if there was anything that she preferred not to discuss, that was her privilege.

She prided herself on being 'smartly' dressed and well groomed. Her manner was bouncy and full of vigour. She was remarkable for her punctuality, in contrast to most of the women. She attempted to paint a picture of an idyllically happy life.

Ginny was raised in the dormitory, although her mother and step-father lived nearby. At the age of twenty-two she married her husband, who was then thirty-seven. 'We just found each other. I was attracted to him and his good nature, and still feel that way after seventeen years of marriage. He's a hard worker and we have had a good life. Mornington Island is home. I like it here.'

She stated that her sexual life was good, and that she obtained satisfaction about half the time. She enjoyed kissing and other fondling. In her own words, 'It is something we both feel happy about. The excitement is early. It takes about five minutes. After it is over, it's good, makes my body feel better. I go to sleep in ten to thirty minutes. It's like taking ether, just puts you off to sleep.' Although she was aged thirty-nine and had four sons, she was not interested in birth control, as she would like to have a little girl to dress up in pretty clothes.

The only concern about sex Ginny expressed was the question of what to tell her teenage sons about getting girls pregnant. She wanted to postpone doing this, but knew she should not. I suggested that this was a matter in which both she and her husband could share responsibility. While she claimed that she and her husband can discuss such things, it apparently had not occurred to her that this was also his responsibility.

While she expressed great satisfaction with her current life, she had other ambitions for herself. She guardedly admitted that she would like to move into one of the new homes that were then being constructed. In addition, she would like a trip around the world, especially to see America.

It was Ginny who suggested further interviews. She clearly saw herself as a colleague of mine, ready to aid in the investigation, volunteering information about other people, and wanting to arrange appointments for me. This occurred at a time when I was experiencing difficulty in getting younger women (eighteen to twenty-five) for interviews. We went through several names, but her reply to each was, 'She's stupid, you won't get anything out of her.'

How might one account for this markedly middle-class, Western attitude? No doubt her own innate intelligence and the Mission influence contributed to this, but her attitude was accentuated by the fact that she had worked as a domestic for previous research groups on the island.

I learned upon my return that Ginny had left the island with a white man who was believed to have sufficient financial resources to support her tastes for nice clothing, housing, and travel. From all reports, she apparently did not experience conflict around her desertion of her husband and three older sons. However, she had wanted to have her youngest son with her. While this behaviour was part of open conversation among the islanders, there was little evidence of censure toward Ginny. Rather, there was sympathy for the husband.

Rose Johns: aged fifty

'It's hard if you don't have kin.'

This thin, plain woman with greying hair was known as one of the 'fighters'. I introduced myself as Rose was leaving the store with her box of groceries, and asked if I might walk with her to her home. She looked surprised, but replied with a gruff yes. I offered to help her carry her load. Her retort was, 'I've been doing this for years and I'm going to keep on doing it.' She carried the box part of the time on her head and part of the time on her left shoulder. In her right hand was a sand shark, about half a metre long. She had caught it by its tail when she found it in a tidal pool, before going to the store. She said she planned to cook it over coals.

In her box I could see laundry soap, tea, flour, beef dripping, a tin of beef stew, and two cans of peaches. When we reached her dwelling she plopped the box and the shark on a table just outside the door. The table contained several plastic bowls which had the leavings of porridge, an open can of powdered milk, and some melted butter. Ants were enjoying the various food remnants. On the ground, both inside and outside I could see pieces of damper: roaches as well as ants were devouring these crumbs which obviously had been there for some time as they appeared to be very dry.

Other objects, either on the table or on the ground under it, included several large, soot-blackened tins, some containing tea leaves and very dark tea-stained water, several unwashed knives, a soot-darkened pot, and a can opener. The dead coals of a fire were close by, as well as miscellaneous pieces of what might be called junk.

Rose brought a blanket from inside, and shook off various bits of paper, food, and dirt as she indicated that we were to sit on it. By glancing inside, I could detect that disarray prevailed. There were three cots, with rumpled clothing as well as blankets heaped on them. I could not tell whether the small, one-room structure contained anything else, except for several large cartons.

Rose quickly abandoned her taciturn manner, and regaled me with information, some of which was quite different from that obtained from others. Living with her were three grandchildren, a boy aged nineteen, and two girls aged seven and nine. She went on to say, 'Their mother lives with a white man on the mainland. All of her children had white fathers. She sends me money from time to time and I get their child endowment money. She would have saved me a lot of trouble if they would have had dark-skinned fathers. Tommy, the boy, is cheeky, says a lot of smart things. A lot of the boys and grown-ups, too, call him "yellow-fellow", 'cause of his colour. That makes me mad. There are a lot of half-whites on this island, but they pick on Tommy. I think it is because we have no family here. We don't belong to any of their family groups, no uncles, aunts or cousins to take up for Tommy, or me, so I have to fight to protect him.

'You see, I was sent here from the mainland when I was fourteen. My mother had died. I went back about four years later to work at a station, and married a bloke from another Mission. He was killed by a bull just three months before Helen, my daughter, was born. I didn't know what to do.

This Mission was the only home I knew; so I came back here to have my baby. I tried working at other stations, but they never liked me to bring a child with me, and I had no one here to look after Helen. It's hard if you don't have relatives to help when you're sick or short of food. I'd get mad when I'd see others take care of their kin, but I certainly am not going to ask for help if no one wants to give it to me. I guess that gave me a sharp tongue.

'Helen was smart, so when she was sixteen the Mission sent her to a school to learn how to use a typewriter. She still works in an office when she is not mixed up with a man. I didn't want her back here; if she ever had wanted to marry a Lardil there would have been a big fight. It would be a wrong-head marriage.

'This kinship business works if you are one of them, but it is bad if you aren't. If a boy steals or gambles, he will get off if the policeman or the Counsellor is a relative. They don't overlook anything my Tommy does. They accuse him of things he doesn't do, and then I really fight.

'Now that they have that canteen with beer, if you are a relative it's easy to get a lot more cans than you're supposed to. It's going to be terrible if the Mornington Islanders start running this place. Those in charge will make sure their families get the good jobs.'

Notes

1. An example of the fear of accusations that have tended to be a part of the petty quarrels that often developed among the people, especially the women.
2. As a psychoanalyst, I could hardly believe my ears when I heard this statement. In light of the theoretical implications of toilet training practices and the anal phase of psychosexual development, I asked myself whether this attitude might not be a factor contributing to Pearl's children having become apparently well organized and responsible people.
3. Adopted: considered to be a member of a Lardil kinship group.
4. The story of 'dark people's customs' as used by the paramour seemed to me to be a seductive 'line' used by a smooth-talking man.
5. Catherine's legal spouse was one of the most respected inhabitants of the island. He was described as being objective and fair in his dealings with all the people.
6. Norman was probably the most flamboyant character on Mornington. As near as I could ascertain, he drank more than any of the middle-aged men (and perhaps more than most of the younger ones).
7. Actually the boy died of acute leukemia. The disease and its fatal course had been thoroughly explained to his parents. The Mission Manager doubted that the family thought sorcery was the cause of the child's death.

11

The Younger Lardil Women

The younger Lardil women, those under thirty, had been raised by their own parents in their village dwellings. The Mornington Island Mission, along with others, had gradually abandoned the dormitory system in the latter 1940s. This was part of the changing philosophy of the Missions, and the government, which considered that the orphanage-like institutions were unnatural, and that children should live with their own parents. The parents of these younger Lardil women were the former dormitory inhabitants.

To replace the dormitory, a co-educational day-school was developed by the Mission. At first the school consisted of just one room. It had been gradually expanded, so that by 1970, the school consisted of seven rooms, attended by all children from age five to sixteen. While the educational programme was modelled after that designed for all pupils living in the State of Queensland, the actual curriculum had been modified and curtailed to be commensurate with the attention span, interests, and motivation of the pupils. Only in more recent years had any qualified teachers been in residence at the Mission.

As a result, the younger Lardil women had been raised by parents for whom a Western-type family situation was an entirely new concept, and they had attended a day-school that offered a relatively limited educational program.

Nancy Davis: aged twenty-eight

'I try to correct my children by getting their attention on something else.'

Nancy Davis, in 1970, was eight months pregnant with her third child. She had been born and raised on the island, as had been her husband, David, aged thirty. Nancy's parents lived nearby in the village, and were considered a respected elder couple. Her husband's parents had died several years previously.

Both Nancy and David were working at different stations on the mainland when their parents had 'arranged' that they should marry; although she was not aware that any 'proper skin-kinship' entered into this decision. Nancy had not been particularly interested in her future husband, but being a dutiful daughter and deciding that he needed a wife, she had married him nine years ago: 'His parents didn't feed him well or look after his clothes. Besides, he was a gentle and good man.'

They had both continued to work on the mainland and had saved their wages. When they had returned to the island, at the time that their first child was of the age to enter school, they had had the money to purchase a house, and to furnish it with a kerosene 'fridge' and a double bed. Her husband had built a table and chairs. He now worked as a carpenter for the Mission. She had worked in the Mission clothing store, and was planning to return to a comparable job as soon as her unborn child was several months old. Her mother would care for her child.

From the appearance of the house and what Nancy reported about their diet and their plans for the future, this couple appeared more organized and industrious than many on the island. It seemed to be a good marriage. But what did Nancy have to say about it? 'It's very hard for me to tell my husband what is on my mind. He won't reply. Maybe I say things that worry him. Sometimes he watches me, like he is jealous.' Marital relations had almost always 'upset me inside', she said, pointing to her chest, 'They hurt me emotionally, not physically. It's been so all during my marriage. I don't know why. Perhaps it's my husband's fault.'

By the time I returned to the island, three years later, Nancy had four children, three girls aged nine, five, and three years, and a new son, aged ten months. Pretty, three-year-old Sandra was with Nancy when she came to the caravan to talk with me. We had tea and biscuits, and Sandra sat quietly looking through some magazines I had. It was not unusual for a young child to remain quiet, with a minimum of squirming or of demands for attention under such circumstances.

Although Sandra only smiled at me, her mother claimed that she talked a lot and could be easily understood. Nancy remembered a woman telling her that one shouldn't talk 'baby talk' to children, but should speak clearly. This Nancy had practiced, and all her girls could speak distinctly. At eleven months Tony was saying mum, ta ta (a common term used in greeting), and making the noise of a truck. I might add that many of the young boys of the island imitated the noise of a truck or a gun in their play, probably heard in the movies frequently shown in the village.

In discussing the children, Nancy said, 'My three girls fight over toys. I correct them sometimes, but my husband tends to spoil the kids. He doesn't like hitting; it might drive a child crazy. I agree that if you hit a child all the time, it would make him silly in the head. Some fathers use swag sticks on their children. I try to correct my children by getting their attention on something else, rather than punishing, like telling them a story, picking them up on my lap, or taking them to visit a relative. But Clara, the oldest, sometimes keeps on crying and carrying on; then I put her under the tap water for several minutes to cool her down. Then, I dry her and she goes to sleep.'

The five-year-old, Oreole, has been 'very difficult to manage. She will say 'aye' meaning yes, but she acts like she has trouble hearing. She acts like she is not good here' (indicating the child's head). The teachers had not mentioned anything concerning problems with this daughter, and it had not occurred to Nancy to discuss this with them.

The infant son, Tony, had two lower teeth. Nancy still continued to nurse him, but she supplemented the breast milk with custard, rice, fish, and occasionally soft bread or damper; otherwise, 'he would crawl and pick up crumbs'. She thought that she would continue nursing him until he decided to stop himself. Sandra had weaned herself when she was about a year old by using the cup and forgetting the breast.

Consistent with the reports of most of the mothers, Nancy had already commenced bowel training with Tony. When she would notice that he was starting to push as if to have a bowel movement, she would put a potty under him. Sandra had been only ten months old when she had learned to use the potty, according to Nancy.

When I attempted to discuss masturbatory activities among children, Nancy tended to deny awareness of this subject. However, she then added, 'If any of the parents knew about it, they certainly would belt them.'

I was interested in learning what traditional beliefs and practices Nancy had continued to observe. According to custom, her father had stayed away from the hospital at the time of her deliveries; however, she did not practice the custom of ritual presentation of her children to him. On the other hand, she hoped to have a 'navel cord' ceremony for her two younger children like the one described earlier by Elsie. To this end she had saved their navel cords. She could not observe this custom for her two elder children, as the cord of the first had been lost, and the cord of the second had been discarded at birth in a mainland hospital.

Another ancient custom, which had been practiced by Nancy's mother for Tony, was that of *dami-dami*, which she pressed and squeezed his head while making a sucking noise with her mouth. This action was to insure that Tony would have a nicely shaped head.

Nancy stated that she did not believe in *puri-puri*, although she had heard others talk about it. She agreed with the notion that some mainland Aborigines might inflict sorcery on a Lardil, if a Lardil should visit among them.

On the subject of kinship, Nancy said that she and her husband had not considered any right-head mates for their children. She expressed the thought that the men the girls selected by free choice might prove to be better husbands than any they, as parents, might choose. The important issue was that the intended husband should be a good worker. In the end, Nancy thought, she would leave any such decision to her husband.

In spite of what sounded like a reasonable family situation, except for dissatisfaction with her sexual life, I heard of difficulties (through village gossip) during my second island visit. Nancy had made a dramatic suicide gesture about a year earlier by jumping off the pier into the mud. Depending on the tide, that could have been a jump of 1 to 3 metres. When I asked Nancy about the incident, she said, 'I was in the hospital just before Tony was born. I was sick, upset, no good in the head. My husband came to the hospital; he had been drinking beer, and said nasty things to me. I got mad with him and said I was going to drown myself. Not that I wanted to; I just wanted him to change his mind. I was so angry, I didn't go back to him for several days.'

I did not press Nancy for more information as to what nasty things he had said. Everyone in the village knew that she had been very friendly with a young Kaiadilt man who subsequently had been sent to another Mission. Earlier in this interview, when speaking of her marriage, she had said, 'I'm an on-and-off person, maybe I should have gotten lost.' No doubt some of her concerns about the above episode were reflected in this statement, which at first I did not understand.

Toward the end of this interview, I read to Nancy the material I had recorded from my 1970 visit, and asked her permission to use the additional information she had just told me, saying that I would omit anything she would wish me not to include. She was pleased with the idea of having something written about her, and could think of nothing that she wished excluded.

I finally brought up the subject of incorporation of the village and wondered what she thought of the idea. To this Nancy replied, 'I have to think everything will go all right, as I am one of the directors.'

Frieda Taylor: aged twenty-five
'I don't have enough to do.'

Frieda was obese, round-faced, with very black skin and kinky hair. Solid and stolid were two adjectives that immediately occurred to me that would describe her. Not only did she readily consent to be interviewed, but appeared an hour earlier than the appointed time.

Her greatest complaint was, 'I don't have enough to do.' She was the only child living at home with her parents, and as Frieda said, 'They can look after themselves.' She was earning a few dollars a week by helping an invalid woman. From ages eighteen to twenty, she had worked on a station, but she was the only Aborigine there; it was lonely and she had returned home. What she did not add was that she had been sent home from the station because she had killed the owner's pet dog, apparently in retaliation for not having been taken into town by her employer.

Frieda related, 'I don't like living in the village. There's nothing to do, no special girl or boy friends. Some girls do such terrible things. Girls from good parents can control themselves with boys, but those with "no good" parents can't control themselves. Once I liked a local boy, but my Mum and Dad didn't, so I had to forget him.'

The interview, which had proceeded in a rather monotonous tone, revealed the attitude of a good, compliant, but resentful daughter. The only time that she broke into a smile was when I asked what she would wish the future to hold for her. To this question she readily replied that she'd like to go out and learn to be a nurse, to marry a man who was truthful and honest like herself, and to have a happy life and a big home.

The sad part of these reasonable wishes was that in all probability none would ever be available to her. She had neither the educational background, initiative nor ability; otherwise she could probably have attempted to further her education earlier. In view of her physical unattractiveness and the lack of men on the island who would meet her parents' standards, she would probably never marry and have the big, happy home. She was vague when I tried to establish whether her parents would approve only of a right-head marriage.

And three years later she was still unmarried, and didn't have enough to do.

Una York: aged twenty-one

'I hate this island.'

Una was a tall, thin, curly-haired young woman of rather striking appearance in spite of having one front tooth missing. She had failed to keep an earlier appointment. When approached again, she reluctantly agreed to talk with me. In view of her open and vehement discourse about her situation during the interview, it was difficult to understand her previous reluctance to talk. I did not ask her about it.

She had lived on an island on the east coast of Australia before coming to Mornington when she was eighteen. After finishing school on her home island at the age of sixteen, she had worked as a domestic at a resort hotel. She had met her Lardil husband when he was visiting on her native island. He had returned to see her at least three times and persuaded her to come with him, first to a northern Australian town to visit her sister, and then to Mornington with him. She had planned to return to her home island, but there was not enough money for air fare: so she stayed on at Mornington, became pregnant and married.

Her husband, Calvin, eight years her senior, was the only married one of the three sons of an older Lardil woman. Concerning her mother-in-law, Una said, 'She wants to hold onto her sons. She treats my husband and my children all right, but she won't speak to me. My husband is a good man; he helps me a lot more than other husbands. He carries water and firewood. When I was sick, he'd bring meals to me at the hospital and take care of the children. It is so difficult for the two of us to get three children (ages three, two and eleven months) to the hospital. The hot sand burns their feet.

'I don't like this place; it is horrible. People fight, and growl, and act like wild dingoes. There almost was a boomerang fight last night about girls going to the bush with boys, and then it turned out that they were with the white men from the boat. I never knew a man until my husband.

'My mother taught me to work from the age of six. These people are so lazy, I'm getting that way. I'd like to get a job.' (But she had not asked for any.) 'Most boys are so lazy; they just grow sitting around the place. My husband knows I'm not happy here, but the problem is to get enough money together to get off the island. You save a couple of dollars a week, and then spend it at Christmas.'

Una had three children and claimed that she would like to have six, but did not want to have anymore in the near future. The nursing sister had put her on the pill after her first child, but she had forgotten to take some and had become pregnant. She said this in a way that implied it was the pill's fault and not the result of her own negligence. When I attempted to discuss the various methods of contraception available to her, her expression was so blank one might have thought she did not hear me. I then asked if she knew about and believed in the traditional belief that a baby resulted from a spirit-child entering a woman.[1] After a moment of reflection, she replied with a definite negation.

Una, a newcomer to the island, expressed the strongest dissatisfaction of any person with whom I had contact. I did not think that all of her displeasure was a projection of her own inner problems, but to a certain extent was based on reality. However, she seemed not to have the ability to plan ahead in a constructive way to diminish or alleviate her current unhappy life situation.

During my return visit, I introduced myself to several people who were waiting to sell their handcrafts to the shop, and one quite attractive young woman said she was Una York. I had not recognized her; she had gained weight. With very little reluctance, she came to the caravan where I was living. We had tea and biscuits together as I read to her the previous material, for which she gave me permission to publish.

She told me that her husband had had surgery on his foot; so he was primarily making bark paintings, which 'produces good money'. Her mother-in-law had become more accepting of her, and she felt more satisfied on the island. However, she said she did not mix a lot with the people, but stayed primarily with her husband and children. Then, spontaneously, she told me that she was on the pill; three children were enough. At one point, I wondered why previously she had been so reluctant to talk about this with me. Her reply was, 'I was shy.'

Concerning the topic of the village incorporation, Una said, 'They'll be climbing up the trees when the Mornington Islanders take over. No young ones know how to run things, and all this drinking and gambling is going to ruin us.' Her husband does not drink or gamble.

Ida Elong: aged fifteen
'I would like to be white.'

This tall, lovely young woman was of mixed racial descent: Chinese, Caucasian, and Aborigine. Her long, straight, neatly brushed hair was dark brown; her skin could be best described as tan. She had a winsome smile and a quiet, reserved manner. From her appearance, it would certainly be difficult to identify her ethnic origins.

She was interviewed at the request of her mother, Catherine Elong. Ida, who had been attending a boarding school on the mainland for the past five years, had written that she was unhappy there and did not want to return to school after the Christmas holiday.

The boarding school had about 160 girls, who were predominantly white. However, the problem that she expressed was that the six black students, full-blooded Aborigines, were giving her a 'hard time'. They taunted her and her best friend, who was half-white, half-Aborigine, with verbal insults and controlled the two girls by threat of beating, and even actual beating. She reported that she had experienced no difficulty with her white classmates. This situation had existed ever since she had gone to that school, but it had distressed her more during the past year.

We discussed several things that might be contributing to her increased sensitivity to the taunts. These included the fact that not only was she negotiating adolescence but also during the past year, her parents had separated. We spoke of the additional problems presented by her mixed racial background. After a period of quiet thoughtfulness, she agreed that she could understand how all these factors were contributing to her unhappiness. Thus, she recognized that her dissatisfaction involved more than being teased at school.

Later, I asked Ida what race she considered herself to be. Again, after a long pause, she said, 'Chinese, but if I had my choice, I would like to be white. I have adopted the white man's way of living.' She wrote me a letter about a month after I had left the island. In this, Ida stated that her holiday was almost over and that she was looking forward to going back to school.

When I returned in 1973, her mother informed me that Ida was living on the mainland, but was not in school. About two years earlier she had transferred to a school in a different small city and had hoped to study nursing eventually. Instead, she quit school to work as an aide in a nursing home. Then a young man came along (or perhaps he had been in the picture all the time), and she had gone to live with him and his parents. Her mother, Catherine, thought he was white; or perhaps one-quarter Aborigine.

When Catherine told me of this, she expressed some disappointment that her daughter had not finished her secondary school education. However, she showed more concern when discussing the possibility that any child of Ida's might be considered white. (See p. 105.) She said that she would be disappointed if Ida and any progeny were to turn their backs on the Aboriginal way of life; however, such a decision would be up to them.

Ida had been considered one of the Islanders who had had a good possibility to complete an education. Some had even expressed the hope that she might return to the island as a sister after she had finished her nursing education. But it was as if disappointment and uncompleted plans were to be expected, or were part of the way of life of these people. No one tended to show marked concern when hopes or plans failed to materialize.

Edith Davis: aged thirty
'I have everything I want.'

Edith, who claimed she had everything she wanted, was most reluctant to be interviewed. Both she and her older sister had managed to give various excuses when approached. When I arrived at the finally agreed upon time, her sister was not in sight. Edith was busy sweeping the ground in front of her house, one of the better-looking, prefabricated dwellings, built off the ground. Edith was obese, with hirsute face and arms in addition to a curly, uncombed mop of hair on her head. She had a sullen facial expression. Four naked children, aged one to five were playing in the vicinity. Only the two-year-old was Edith's; the five-year-old was supposed to be entertaining the younger ones during the interview.

Edith had been born and raised on the island, but had met her Lardil husband ten years ago while she was living at a mainland station with her parents. They decided to marry, and she became pregnant. They returned to the island to have a church wedding, for which Edith wore a long white dress and had a bridesmaid. She and her husband went back to the mainland and lived on a station for the next six years, returning only in order to send their older children to school, there being none available at the station.

From Edith's point of view, the marriage had gone well: 'The one thing we argue about is money. He thinks I spend too much on clothes, and I lose my temper when he gambles.' When I asked when was the last time she had lost her temper, her reply was, 'Last night, he said he was going for water, but he didn't come back; instead he went gambling. He's a good drinker; he doesn't go wild, or get silly.'

I asked if there was anything she wished for, and received the amazing response, 'I have everything I want: all my children, and a good home.' When I rather teasingly suggested that she might wish her husband would stop gambling, she laughed for the first time and said, 'I don't think he will; anyway, he doesn't make a habit of it'.

The marriage had produced five children, aged ten, eight, seven, four, and two. She claimed that she had had her family, and did not want any more babies. When I asked how she was going to prevent having babies, she was silent and developed a blank expression. When I suggested that she could seek help concerning birth control from the nursing sisters, and attempted to explain the methods available, she continued to be non-responsive. She showed what seemed to be an absolute lack of interest in, or understanding of contraception. She ended the topic by claiming, in an adamant manner, that she just wasn't going to have any more children.

In view of her previous reluctance to talk to me, I was surprised upon my return to the island when Edith spontaneously came up to me to re-introduce herself. She was very talkative and volunteered a great deal of information. She had had another child, her sixth. Her sister, who had successfully eluded being interviewed by me, had died on 1 January, 1972, after a day's illness (acute nephritis). Edith had assumed the care of her sister's five children. In addition, in order to make extra money, she was working at the hospital laundry. Her husband was away working at a cattle station. She responded in a warm, friendly way when

I expressed my amazement that she could care for eleven children and work at the same time. She volunteered that her mother was a great help. At that moment, she pointed to her old mother who, along with three nude children, was sound asleep under a nearby tree.

Whenever I would see Edith around the village or hospital, we would have a congenial exchange. In contrast to her previous denial of any interest in contraception, she spontaneously told me that she was 'taking the pill'.

Three Young Women

While I had experienced little difficulty in obtaining cooperation in interviewing the women over thirty years of age, those in their late teens or early twenties were particularly elusive. Finally, with the help of an older sister, I was able to see three young women together. Edna, aged sixteen; her sister Rose, twenty-one; and Wilma, twenty; constituted the group. All had unkempt hair, but clean, unironed dresses. All were wearing some sort of make-shift jewellery, including rubber discs removed from oil drums. One had her eyebrows plucked out to a fine line, very unusual among the women on the island. None were working, and all three were reputed to be the most promiscuous girls in the village; however, none had had any children. I offered them fruit juice and cigarettes, which they readily accepted; but it was evident that they felt extremely ill at ease with me. About this time Elsie Roughsey appeared unexpectedly. With obvious relief, they asked her to stay.

In spite of the supportive urging given them by Elsie and myself, almost every question, ranging from what they had done earlier in the day, to what they might wish for themselves, was met with either giggles or silence. With a lot of help from Elsie, Wilma was able to say that she had spent eighteen months at another Mission, receiving training in dressmaking and cooking, but that she had not used anything she had been taught. Rose once worked for three months at a station, but could give no explanation about why she had returned to the island. Edna, the youngest one, who seemed slightly less hesitant in expressing her thoughts, mentioned that she would like to go to the mainland to work as a domestic. When the subject of boyfriends or marriage was introduced, only giggles resulted, and not very enthusiastic ones at that.

Probably the three related very little in a verbal way to any adult; however, the social distance from me that they felt added to the difficulty in developing any reasonable exchange. These were some of the girls to whom Ginny Cole had referred as 'stupid'. They were in the group that Una York hinted had caused a disturbance by going off in the bush with boys. Their degree of immaturity and lack of motivation for any task was marked. There certainly was little available for them in the way of work or recreation on the island.

Three years later, at age nineteen, Edna was married to a boy whom she had met while on holiday at another Mission, and was living there. Rose, aged twenty-four was married to a local fellow, and the mother of a child. Winnie, twenty-three, was about five months pregnant. She wanted to marry the young Lardil who had impregnated her, but he was not interested. Apparently, because of this, many arguments and fights marked their relations.

So, at least two of these young women had reached the status of being married women. Becoming mothers also gave them some financial support through the various government allotments. In this way they had meshed into the local community.

Louise Rose: aged twenty-three

'I'd like a big house on Denham Island.'

Louise was a slender Lardil, who worked in the Mission office. Efficient and conscientious in keeping the financial accounts, she also practised typewriting, with some instruction from one of the school teachers. She hoped that this skill would enable her to leave the island, and to obtain clerical work on the mainland. Previously, she had worked as a domestic at a station for approximately a year. She had returned to live with her parents when she was five months pregnant. The father of the baby was a half-caste who also worked at the station. He was already married. Louise reported this in a matter-of-fact way, without embarrassment or rancour.

Louise's father was a pensioner. Her parents, four unmarried siblings, Louise and her baby all lived in the same dwelling. Her baby girl was readily accepted into the family. Three married siblings, who had a total of thirteen children, lived in their own houses.

Before I had left the island in 1970, Louise had already contacted a government officer whose duty was to help Aborigines continue their education or to secure employment on the mainland. She was planning to leave her child, then aged three, with her parents. Some months later, I received a letter from her, saying she was pregnant and was planning to marry the baby's father, a white man who was working on one of the prawn trawlers plying the Gulf waters.

However, when I returned in 1973, she had two daughters and no husband. She was again pregnant by another white man who was working on one of the fishing boats. Louise said, 'This man supplies me with money; none of the others did. He is kind and wants to adopt my two other children when we marry. He is going to build a house on Denham Island. He plans to teach the local boys how to make nets and other things for commercial fishing. We will have a lovely home.' She wanted six children, so she had no interest in birth control.

I asked Louise if anyone had objected to her going with white men. She was not aware of any criticism. This was verified when I asked others about this. The opinion expressed was that they felt sorry for her, because they thought this man would desert her as had the previous men. They knew that she wished to marry, and thought she would make a good wife. No one could offer an explanation as to why she had become involved with white men, instead of local men. Louise, herself, said, 'white men are kinder and make more money'. Later information from the island confirmed the prediction that this white man would also desert her. He had left the Gulf area.

Notes

1. It has been considered that the Aborigines did not understand the biology of conception. Accordingly the father only played a spiritual role, not a physiological one. A man would have a vision or a dream that a spirit-child (often symbolizing his totem) would enter his wife's womb. Later the woman might dream this also and know she was with child. However, I was not able to ascertain that this remained as a viable concept of the Islanders: all seemed aware of the biological aspects of paternity. The Reverend Douglas Belcher reported that one older man claimed that his son could not have impregnated a girl as it was necessary to have sexual relations on three occasions before pregnancy could result and his son had performed the act only twice with her.

12
The Kaiadilt Women

The material presented so far has mainly dealt with the Lardil, the tribe indigenous to Mornington Island, with some information concerning those who were brought from the mainland as children, or who came more recently as a result of marriage. Brief mention has been made of the Kaiadilt, a tribe evacuated from their native island of Bentinck in 1948, when they were found to be on the brink of annihilation.

Bentinck Island, consisting of approximately 130 square kilometres plus surrounding reefs, located some 30 kilometres southeast of Mornington Island, is essentially out of sight of any other land area. In 1802 Lieutenant Matthew Flinders of the Royal Navy, while exploring the Gulf of Carpentaria, named this island for Bentinck, the Governor of Madras.[1] In the intervening years, there had been no sustained contact with any other groups of people, white, Aboriginal, or Malaysian, who occasionally crossed the waters of the southern part of the Gulf.

Gully Peters and a few other Mornington people had established tenuous contact with the Bentinck Islanders during their fishing expeditions starting in the 1920s. The Kaiadilt were described as being elusive and hostile to those attempting to make any overtures to them.

In 1947 the missionary, the Reverend J. B. McCarthy, Gully Peters and several other Lardil visited Bentinck Island and found the people to be in great physical, and probably emotional distress. They persuaded a small group of Kaiadilt to return with them to Mornington, where they were fed and made to feel safe from the inter-hordal killings. After some months they were returned to Bentinck for the purpose of telling their fellow islanders how it was to live on Mornington. Finally, in 1948, with the help of the Mornington Island people, all were evacuated from

Bentinck by the Mission.

Several studies of the Kaiadilt by Tindale have given important background information concerning these most isolated people.[2] They were divided into eight territorially defined hordes, called *dolnoro*. From a population of 103 persons in 1910, they gradually increased to a maximum of 123 in 1942. Five years later there were fifty-eight surviving on Bentinck before removal to Mornington Island. Tindale gave the following factors as contributing to this catastrophic decline in population after 1942:[3] growth of population beyond the limit of capacity of the area; conflict between the hordes; climatic change (drought); and catastrophies (tidal waves and mass drowning). As a result of these factors there were inter-hordal killings of adult males and females, fewer births, more infant deaths, deaths from weakening, especially of older women, and drownings when escape to Allen Island (some 13 kilometres to the west) was attempted on very primitive rafts.

When Dr John Cawte and I questioned the Kaiadilt men and women now living on Mornington Island concerning the difficulties they experienced while on Bentinck, these informants emphasized the fighting, and insisted that it was 'over women'.[4] They were adamant

Kaiadilt women and children resting in the shade

that this strife was for satisfaction of sexual desire rather than to gain social status or to give more economic security. Each perceived fighting and sex, but did not relate these to the basic ecological difficulties.

In an article reporting a genetic survey of the Aboriginal populations of the Wellesley Islands, Simmons, Tindale and Birdsell made a number of interesting observations about the Kaiadilt. These observations are summarized as follows:

> They possess unique blood grouping.[5] The hair of the children is either blonde or light brown with lighter tips. With ageing, the hair of the women becomes tawny to dark brown in colour; that of the men becomes dark brown.
>
> Bentinck Islanders had not mixed with other Aborigines, and may be regarded as a classic example of shore and reef-dwelling people with a palaeolithic tradition. From the microevolutionary point of view their probable pre-history suggests that they were derived from the adjacent mainland Aborigines. Environmental factors point to an ancestral group rafting on Bentinck for about 3500 years.
>
> The Kaiadilt lacked all traces of the eight subsection kinship class, which the Lardil had incorporated through their contact with mainland Aborigines. In their mythology, their dance patterns, and in their music, the Bentincks were far removed from all their neighbours. Another fact that distinguished them is that they did not have the dingo, the dog possessed by all other Aborigines. While the Kaiadilt and Lardil languages were somewhat dissimilar, it was possible for each group to understand the other.[6]

Tindale reported that there were both inter-hordal and intra-hordal marriages, probably on a one-to-one exchange basis, except when the women were taken and held as a result of killing.[7] However, such stealings were likely to have been balanced out, since the male of one *dolnoro* was likely to be killed in revenge for the death of a man of the other. In four of the groupings, intra-hordal mating was not merely accepted; it was sanctioned. Married women and their children lived with members of the husband's horde. On the death of a husband, the wife would pass to her husband's eldest son, or to her husband's brother, whichever was older, or she might be claimed by a man in another territorial group.

After many years of living as one of the most isolated groups of Aborigines and existing on the edge of annihilation, how did the Kaiadilt appear to the Lardil of Mornington, who had been exposed to Western influence for about thirty years? To quote Elsie Roughsey, 'When they first came, they were naked for three to six years. Each group would be in one humpy. They would have one child right after another. To wild people, sex is nothing. They'd do it right in their own camp, they had no shame. Children didn't take notice, or else thought it was the thing to be done.

'They would put mud all over everyone; they even rubbed their bowel movement over their bodies. They smeared dugong or turtle blood over themselves. Maybe they dirtied themselves and their children, so that no one would go near their camp. Maybe this was to keep others from having sex with them.'

At first Elsie was 'frightened by them; they looked so fearsome. Gradually I went to their camp and would bathe some of their children, but when I'd go back, they'd be dirty all over again.' She thought that they would marry first or second cousins or whoever took them. She did not know anything about the Bentinck religion.

She reported that when a Bentinck was sick, their own kind would not care for him, but the Lardil would go to nurse and feed a Bentinck who was ill. This was confirmed by others. This may have reflected the Lardil practice of sharing with their extended family grouping, as well as the Mission teachings. The disinclination of the Kaiadilt to look after their own sick possibly resulted from a loss of empathy as a result of their desperate situation on Bentinck.

During the early years following the arrival of the Kaiadilt, many of the Lardil couples would 'adopt' a Bentinck family, especially if they shared the same totemic symbol. They made some attempt to think of the newcomers as part of their extended kinship grouping. However, with few exceptions, the two tribes have remained socially apart, even though the Bentinck camp has been directly adjacent to the main village area. Although the children have gone to school together, inter-mingling has been minimal in this situation. Gully Peters used to go weekly to the Bentinck area and would hold a Christian service in the Kaiadilt tongue. However, few have attended church or have shown little inclination to espouse Christianity. The social exclusion, as well as a desire to keep to themselves, has tended to keep the Bentincks from becoming more involved in church activities or other aspects of village life.

Very gradually their housing improved, but even as late as 1966, when the New South Wales field survey unit was on the island, the Kaiadilt continued to live primarily in 'humpies' (brush shelters).[8] By 1970, all had corrugated iron huts, usually consisting of one room only. Although each had a closed pan-type toilet, it was reported that faeces could be found on the ground inside the shacks. However, during the evacuation precipitated by the outbreak of hepatitis in 1970, visits to the temporary camps showed the Bentinck group had built a more adequate type of toilet in their area than had most of the Lardil.

Some of the Mission staff reported that they felt that the Kaiadilt were more reliable workers than the Lardil. They were more likely to appear when expected, and were less likely to grumble or become hostile about menial or routine tasks.

I had difficulty in establishing an interview situation with most of the Kaiadilt women during my initial visit to the island. When I was in their camp area, I was reminded of Elsie's comment about them when they first came to Mornington Island. She had been 'frightened by them', she said, 'they looked so fearsome'. The middle-aged women continued to have a fearsome appearance; their voices had the tonal quality of anger. At one point, I persuaded them to perform their Bentinck dance while I was making a movie. The dance consisted of exaggerated stomps which, when viewed through the zoom lens of my camera, appeared war-like.

The following material was written about the Kaiadilt women after my contact with them in 1970.

The Middle-Aged Women

There were thirteen Kaiadilt women in the age range of thirty-five to sixty (aged ten to thirty-five when they left Bentinck). There were five Kaiadilt women past age sixty, but communication with them was all but impossible. Indeed, superficial mental examinations, performed with the help of younger interpreters, suggested impairment in memory and orientation.

Those in the middle-age range all had a rather untamed look. They appeared dishevelled, with matted hair and dirty clothing which was often torn, consequently exposing their breasts. Many have scars on their head and extremities from self-inflicted wounds.[9] These women were extremely thin, even emaciated. They had little command of English. During our talks, when the women would become very excited about what they were saying, even their daughters who were translating for me had difficulty in following them. The emotion they displayed was labile and unpredictable. In addition to having to use as interpreters the younger women, who were somewhat reluctant to act in this capacity, there was always a flock of children around wanting to be involved in the conversation. Any sort of privacy was impossible. Needless to say, the information from these women is incomplete, but I have chosen two as being representative.

Olly: aged fifty
'We left Bentinck because of fighting'.

The following is the story related by fifty-year-old Olly:[10] 'We left Bentinck to go to Allen Island because of the fighting. My husband was a great fighter, but he was the only man left in our part of the island.

The others had been killed by men from the eastern part of the island. My husband killed his nephews because they were breaking or stealing his raft, just to make trouble. They'd try to harm women. We left for Allen Island on a raft, without any food, but we had rubbing sticks to make fire. We were glad to get to Allen as there was enough water, and food such as crabs, wild potatoes, goannas and berries. We made bush shelters against the wind.'

Olly had five children: one born on Bentinck, two on Allen, one at Aurukun, and one soon after her arrival at Mornington.[11] She claimed that her husband never hit her, that he loved her and was good to her. 'My husband and I wanted to get married, we needed each other.' Olly explained that it was customary before a marriage for fights to break out between families. She continued, 'He had to prove what a man he was. He had to fight my father and brothers. They threw spears.' Actually, he had fought her step-father, since her own father had died. Her father had had four or five wives. Her own husband had three wives, but Olly was the first. Olly claimed that she was glad her husband had other wives. They gave her companionship and also she could stay in the camp while the other two wives went hunting with him. When they came home, each wife cooked her own food. She insisted that there was no jealousy among the wives, and that they never got into fights because they were too scared of their husband. Besides, they were relatives; therefore, there was no jealousy. (During all this her daughter, Linda, aged thirty, and several other young women were giggling among themselves, as if quite titillated by this information.)

Olly said that they each had a separate camp and the husband visited each in turn for sex. She claimed she was 'shy' with her husband. When asked if she was shy with us, her reply was, 'no, we are all ladies'.

Lena: aged forty-eight

Lena, about forty-eight years of age, gave the following information: 'We came to Mornington because the Missionary wanted us to, and we wanted to leave Bentinck because we were afraid of the fighting. I don't know what the wars were about; they just fought. My first husband drowned in a raft accident.' She had had one daughter by this man, Winnie (aged thirty), who was still living with her mother. When Lena's first husband had drowned, she had gone to live with her father and brothers, who were great fighters. According to her, her father had had ten wives. Lena's mother was his second wife. Lena later married 'Old Jack', and they came to Mornington Island together in 1948. Lena, in contrast to Olly, said that her father's wives would get jealous of each other at times. They wanted to be near him; some would stay in camp, some would go hunting.

In speaking of illness, Lena said that the Kaiadilt did not have wise men who acted as healers. Rather, when sickness occurred, it was customary to make a fire with green leaves from a special vine. The sick would sit near the fire to breathe the aroma of the burning leaves, which acted as a medicine. Lena attempted to tell about how sorcery was practiced on Bentinck; however, she became so excited that her daughter was not able to translate and I was never able to get Lena back on the subject again. She spoke of the belief that people would dream of birds when someone was going to die, and that the person's ghost or spirit went to the East when he died. As nearly as I was able to understand, this concept was similar to that of the Lardil.

Lena stated that the Kaiadilt women knew that babies resulted from having sexual relations with men. When a women was pregnant, she would eat only small fish. When the baby was about to be born, they would make a nest of leaves on the ground for it. She said that in giving birth, 'the women would dance with pain; some would swing from trees'. They were helped by their mother or aunties to give birth to the baby, but the cord was cut by a male cousin.[12] He would put the cord in a basket, dig a hole, and bury the cord in the basket. If breast milk did not come, they pressed 'milk' out of a root into the woman's nipple and this caused the milk to flow. They would rub the baby with fish fat to give it strength and energy.

These women denied that there had been a serious lack of food or water on Bentinck Island. They agreed that the inter-hordal fighting was the reason for leaving the island, but they could shed no light on the question of what the fighting was all about.

Three Unmarried Kaiadilt Women
'We love our parents better than the man.'

It had been difficult to talk with the middle-aged Kaiadilt women because of their poor command of English, the reluctance of the younger women to act as interpreters, and the utter confusion created by so many children milling around. I had anticipated better success with the younger ones. When I attempted to arrange interviews with three somewhat younger women of this group, I again encountered some resistance. Because of the lack of privacy, which prevailed at the Kaiadilt enclave, I wanted to talk with them elsewhere. They were not willing to come to the Mission house: eventually I was able to meet them on three occasions under a tree behind the church. Their reluctance to be interviewed seemed to be based on their feelings of social distance from me which engendered a passive type of hostile avoidance.

These three were all about thirty years of age, unmarried, and had a total of eight children. Two of the women were employed as nurses aides at the hospital, while the third was unemployed and apparently living on the government assistance received for her four children. This third one, Winnie, had been hospitalized on the mainland twice for lengthy periods for tuberculosis. The others, Cathy and Linda, had from time to time worked as domestics on stations. This explained why some of their children were half-white. Linda lived with her mother, Olly; Winnie lived with her mother, Lena. Both of Cathy's parents were dead and she had made her home with a Lardil couple who had befriended her father.

All three young women were dressed in a manner comparable to the Lardil. They went barefooted and wore clean, cotton unironed dresses which they had purchased in the Mission clothing store. All had good command of English. Winnie was reported to have been the brightest in her class when she was in school; but she refused an opportunity to continue an education on the mainland. She had a pensive, if not depressed, countenance.

Cathy was the only one who openly expressed a wish to marry. There was a Kaiadilt man, five years her junior, to whom she felt that she was 'engaged'. The big problem was her fiance's mother, whom the three described as a 'wicked old woman and a witch'. This woman wanted all three of her sons at home at all times. When they would leave to go hunting or visiting, she would growl when they returned. She would go into a rage if she saw the one son talking with Cathy. The idea seemed to be that it was fun for Cathy to fantasy getting married to this man, but that the likelihood of its happening was minimal.

The other two, Linda and Winnie, felt that marriage was not a possibility for them. According to their count, in the Bentinck camp there were eleven women of marriageable age and only four men.[13] During the past year, only one Kaiadilt girl had married, and that was to a mainlander. One Bentinck man also had married a mainlander, but his mother continued to fuss with the son when he visited her, and would have nothing to do with his wife.

What these three young women said regarding the older Kaiadilt people's attitude toward marriage could be summarized as follows: Their parents and relatives approved of no man. They would rather help their daughters to raise their grandchildren than have the daughters marry. Parents want them home to look after them. They depend on their grown children, sons as well as daughters, for money, water, cooking, and taking them around. In return, they care for the grandchildren while the daughters work or fish. They make a 'fuss' when they become pregnant, but they do not want them to marry the child's father. The young women concluded, 'We love our parents better than the man.' They said they were not disillusioned by men, although they saw much jealousy, fighting, and desertion of wives. All of this was said in a most matter-of-fact manner, as if it was un-changeable. No obvious resentment was expressed.

An example of a family grouping was that of Olly's, which included Linda and her two offspring; Olly's other daughter, Charlotte (aged twenty-four) and her two children; and three sons, aged thirty-five, twenty-five, and seventeen, none of whom were married. The women and children all slept in a one-room structure, while the three brothers slept in another. Linda had no idea why her three brothers had not married; the subject had apparently never arisen. She knew they were very dependent on their mother. However, she thought that if her mum were to die, the boys would leave and never come back to the island. She was quite vague about what she and her sister would do.

What could account for this negative attitude about marriage? Linda and Winnie were the offspring of mothers who were born and raised in a polygynous society. Also, a careful reading of Tindale's genealogies reveals that most of the mothers had borne children fathered by more than one man. As nearly as could be ascertained, marriage as known among Europeans did not exist in the original Kaiadilt society. Marriage meant which man claimed which woman, perhaps after killing the man who had previously claimed her. In addition, the Kaiadilt, especially the older ones, were for the most part socially separated from the predominant Lardil group and their culture, even though the physical proximity was very close. Therefore, marriage in the Western sense had not become a part of the middle-aged Kaiadilt's way of life. Possibly a factor that contributed to Cathy's wish to marry, was that both of her parents were dead, so she was free now to attempt to set up her own family unit, in keeping with the European customs prevailing on Mornington.

Also, there appeared to be marked mutual dependence among the parents, especially the mothers, and their adult offspring. This was probably accentuated in this group by the fact that they had undergone a type of deprivation that led them to the brink of extinction. Their excessive mutual dependency may have reflected the gross stress and social disorganization they had experienced on Bentinck. The discrimination by the dominant Lardil perhaps accentuated an intra-group cohesion and dependency among the Kaiadilt.

Carrie Ides: aged thirty-four
'They'd appreciate it.'
Carrie was born in about 1936 on Bentinck Island, so that she was

about twelve years old when she, along with the rest of the Kaiadilt tribe, was evacuated to Mornington Island in 1948.

When I first arrived on the island, she had been pointed out as a possible interpreter for any of the Kaiadilt who spoke little English. When I approached her concerning this possibility, I received only a sullen, negative reaction. However, I had continued to greet her casually; and utimately, I decided to ask for an interview at a time when I was interested in talking with several of the women who had accepted the use of a contraceptive device. She immediately agreed. It soon became evident why she had been unresponsive to my request for her help as interpreter: her own command of English was very limited.[14]

When I had casually observed her, I had thought that she seemed better organized than most of the Kaiadilt women. For example, the manner in which she went about her grocery shopping, and what she purchased, indicated more efficiency and judgment. She came for the interview (bringing her two youngest children with her), in a bedraggled dress and with her reddish-black curly hair matted. There were several scars on her arms and face which she said were from wounds, self-inflicted while she was still a child on Bentinck Island. She said that this was a custom like *nurri-nurri*, but she could no longer recall the specific sadness or sickness that had prompted her to perform the act.

The interview proceeded in a painfully slow manner because of her limited knowledge of English. Among other things, I wanted to get her views on contraception. Carrie had five children. She had felt so sick after the last one was born that she had gone to the nursing sister to ask for some method of birth control. She had previously learned from two other women that contraceptive devices were available. Since she had been using one she had felt much better.

Carrie's husband did not have regular work, but he hunted (fished) a great deal, and Carrie worked in the hospital laundry two days a week to eke out a living. During the interview, I was impressed by the sincerity of this impoverished woman, who seemed to be trying so hard to be a responsible person, with such limited resources of any type. When I attempted to find out what she might wish or hope for herself, with great thoughtfulness and difficulty she formulated the idea that she would wish for people to be more helpful to one another; especially to help the old people. I told her that I had heard from others that she was the only 'niece' that looked after some of the older Kaiadilt.

At the end of the meeting, I gave her some biscuits for her children and some dried fruit to take to the old people. Her reply was, 'They'd appreciate it.' Something about Carrie, her humble sincerity and an air of pathos, made me feel more compassion for her than I had felt for anyone else. Some people have so much; some, so little.

The Kaiadilt Women in 1973

Upon my return three years later, without much effort I was able to establish relaxed and really quite friendly relations with at least three of the Kaiadilt women. Had time allowed, I am sure that I would have been able to accomplish the same with others. During this second visit I noticed perhaps six or more Kaiadilt in church; I had not observed any there previously. The physical appearance of their area was unchanged, and only one family had moved to a new house by the airstrip.

One day, Nancy Waxler and I walked through the Bentinck area at a time when it was deserted: everyone was apparently working, or had gone to the store, and the children were all in school. There was one woman, of indeterminate age, remaining. She came out of a tent, and screamed and screamed at us, apparently in the Kaiadilt tongue. We thought that we could understand one word of what she said: money. We assumed that this one English word had definite meaning to her.

In marked contrast to this screaming woman was Clara, a most poised and gracious Kaiadilt. No one had suggested that I talk with her during my earlier visit. I only learned of Clara's existence several months before returning to Mornington Island, while visiting in London one of the nursing sisters who had been at the Mission in 1970. Clara proved to be an excellent informant.

Clara: aged thirty-eight

'We like to live with our own people.'

Clara was twelve years old when she was brought to Mornington Island. She then had several years of schooling, with Dick Roughsey as teacher. When she was twenty-two (in 1957), she had gone to the mainland to work as a domestic, and had remained there almost continuously for ten years; she became quite versed in Western thought and manners. She had not married, but had had two children, a son, aged nine and a daughter, aged five. According to Clara, the fathers of each child were 'half-castes'.

Clara had returned to the island in 1968 in order that her son could go to school. She had worked for a while in the hospital laundry, but in 1973 was employed as the domestic in the home of one of the Mission staff and his wife. I first interviewed her in their house at a time when her daughter was playing with the one-year-old daughter of her employers. The two children played nicely together, and whenever they demanded attention Clara would divert them by giving them a different toy to play with or a book to look through.

At age thirty-eight, Clara was rather plump and still had some tawny colouration to her hair. She was neatly groomed and dressed. She was proud of her house in which she and her two children lived. She had ordered the materials and had employed two carpenters to build it. It was set about a metre off the ground, had at least two rooms, and had louvred windows. She obtained her water from a village tap, and chopped her own wood for an open fire. Her monthly income was approximately $102.00 of which $12.00 was from child endowment and the remainder from her twenty-six-hour week.

What was Clara's daily routine? She and her children would arise at six. She would prepare breakfast (typically tea and damper), and do some chores around the house. Then she would spend a social hour in the vicinity of the hospital before going to her employer's house at eight o'clock. She would return home to prepare the noon meal, which, on the first day that we met, consisted of bullock meat, onions, and gravy. Two afternoons a week she would return to her employer's from two to five o'clock. The other afternoons she could do as she wished; such as go fishing. For the evening meal, on the day of our interview she was planning to have bacon, eggs, and fruit (apples and oranges). Ordinarily she would put the children to bed at nine o'clock and would retire at the same time. If there were a movie show in the village she would usually attend this.

In talking about the past, Clara recalled being brought to Mornington Island on a big, white boat named *Dolphin*. She, together with about nine women and children and six men, had been living on Sweers Island just east of Bentinck. They would go back and forth between these two islands by raft. The men would hunt turtle, dugong, and fish. The women would get fish from under the rocks with their bare hands. They would find turtle eggs, roots, potatoes, and wild figs. They used sticks to start fires, and there was plenty of water.

She continued, 'The people used to be bad, killing each other, when I was a kid. An older woman told me they'd kill for women. There would be unhappy times when people would kill each other, especially at night. I was scared. The happy part was that there was plenty of meat and berries. There used to be a lot of dancing, particularly at night.' Then she described the dance, which was the stomp that I had filmed previously.

Clara said her parents had died when she was young. Her father had died about 1945 by drowning in a raft accident. Clara would have been eleven. Her mother also had drowned during a raft trip between Bentinck and Allen Island. This had occurred just prior to Clara's being brought to Mornington Island. She was then 'adopted' by her mother's sister, who lated died on Mornington. Clara said that she now thought of Aunt Lena as her stepmother and Uncle Jack as her step-father.

I was interested in obtaining other information concerning customs of the Bentincks prior to their abandonment of their island. She did not seem to have much or any awareness of a kinship system, or of the *dolnoros* (hordes) as delineated by Tindale. She thought the Kaiadilt had an expression comparable to 'cousin-brothers', but that they did not use it.

At first Clara denied knowing about the practice of 'being promised' to a man. Later, she contradicted herself when I asked what constituted a Bentinck marriage. Her description of this was as follows: 'The parents took the woman to the man's camp when the girl was of marriage age (nine or ten years old). It had been arranged when the girl was born and she was promised to the man. When the young girl was taken to the man's camp, the older wives would growl and hit and bite her, but the man would hit the older wives for being nasty to the young girl. Husbands were very bossy. The young girl usually looked after the children while the older women and the man went hunting.' Clara said that she had not been promised to anyone. She could give no reason for this, except that she had been a little girl when her parents had died (actually she was about eleven).

Clara reported that when people would die on Bentinck, women, men, and children would all cry. She could not describe any sort of burial ceremony, and was not aware of any belief that the spirit went to the East after death (as reported by Lena and some Lardil).

She spoke of the self-infliction of wounds, which the Bentinck women have continued to practice up to the present day when they experience anxiety or sorrow. They called it *njiltanjilt*. Using stones or bailer shells, they hit their head, arms, legs or other parts of the body until they bled. These scars were different from the four linear scars that Clara and others had on their upper arms. The linear scars are called *porkant*, and were inflicted on babies by the older people to make the girls grow into big women; the boys, strong men. Some of the older men used to make cuts and rub mud into them to produce designs on their bodies (cicatices); but none have continued this practice on Mornington.

Clara stated, 'My totem is the dugong (in the Kaiadilt tongue, *bija*). It's my dream: my father and mother gave it to me. It was my father's totem and his father's totem; I will pass it on to my children. It's our "bush" name. We can eat our totem.'

She was quite verbal about sorcery *(kalwnet)* as practiced on Bentinck. The sorcerer might use bones of fish or other animals, or the poison wood of the lava tree to kill a victim. The ritual involved in sorcery might be as follows: The sorcerer would place the lava tree wood among some rocks, and would start a fire. When it was red hot, a bone would be placed in the fire and covered with grass. When the first burned out, the whole thing would be buried under sand. Then in two or three weeks the intended victim would feel pain all over, would become constipated, and would be unable to pass water. The family would burn leaves and grass as medicine in an attempt to make the victim better; but often, Clara said, 'she couldn't be made better; she'd die'. After the victim's death, the family would have a big fight, day and night. They'd try to identify the sorcerer by his or her footprints. As Clara told this, it seemed that sorcery was primarily between women. She then clarified the insinuation by saying, 'Women did this to each other because of having to share their husbands, they wanted the man for themselves.'

Almost the moment that Clara had finished telling about sorcery, with much emotional involvement, my associate, Nancy Waxler, came to the house. With both ease and grace, Clara shifted into the role of a Western hostess. She served us coffee and cake, and we engaged in casual tea-time conversation. Clara told of catching about a dozen fish the previous afternoon, which she had fried and shared with the other people in the Bentinck camp. I expressed interest in joining her for fishing, and she seemed pleased with the idea.

In a later interview with Clara, she claimed that the Bentinck work harder than the Mornington Islanders. She felt that the latter regarded work as too hard for them, or that they did not like a particular job.[15] She went on to say: 'We like to live with our own people; Mornington Islanders are trouble makers. I don't know what will happen if the people take over the running of the island. There will be a lot of fighting. The old Bentincks are planning to go back to our island.

'Five Bentincks and two Lardil have been back on Bentinck Island for a month. They are starting gardens. The man running the turtle farm is helping them. I don't know if I'd go back to Bentinck Island or not.

'About fifteen years ago, some of us and a few of the Mission staff went there on a holiday. It seemed strange. There was plenty of water and swamp grass. We caught big turtles. There were so many fish on the reef that all we had to do was to pull in the lines. There were two kinds of wild potatoes.'

Clara seemed to have no objection to the idea of returning and having only bush food to eat. In further discussing a possible migration of her people back to their native island, I raised the question of what they would do without nursing sisters or school teachers. To this she had no answer. It was likely that these considerations had not entered her thoughts, or perhaps were of no importance, in that the Kaiadilt had lived on Bentinck Island for many centuries, perhaps 3500 years,[16] without developing these roles in their society.

During the interviews, and our fishing trip, Clara was poised and open. She was obviously intelligent and an excellent informant.

However, when I asked what wishes she might have (for herself, her children, and her people) she appeared completely blocked in her thinking. It was as if she could not avail herself of the privilege of fantasy.

Socializing With the Kaiadilt

During the first Sunday evening after my return to Mornington, Elsie, Dick, and I walked through the Bentinck area of the village. We greeted the various people who were sitting around eating fish, or just lounging and doing nothing. I asked about Linda and Winnie, who were pointed out to me. When I turned in their direction, they started giggling and walking away from me towards the water. Since I followed them to the water's edge, they had little possibility of eluding me. After some superficial conversation, I asked whether they remembered our previous talks as being difficult, and whether they would be interested in chatting again. They both agreed it had been hard; but Winnie consented to take me to the turtle farm where she was working.

A week later I walked into the area again with some scraps of meat, mostly gristle, left over from stew that I had made from bullock meat. I asked Linda if anyone had a dog, intending to offer the meat scraps for this animal. Linda informed me that no Kaiadilt had a dog, as one must obtain them from the mainland and have them registered.[17] I was a little perplexed as to what to do with the meat scraps. I felt it might be in-sulting to offer them to Linda when I had obviously meant them for a dog. I asked where Clara's house was located. When I reached her place and called for her, she came to the door with a newspaper in her hand, which she mentioned she had been reading. I asked whether she or someone else might have some use for the meat; she quickly accepted it.

I then said that I was going to take a walk down the beach, and Clara volunteered to come with me. Then Winnie and four children also decided to join us. As we started our jaunt, some teen-aged boys were saying something about me in a teasing manner. Winnie volunteered the content of their teasing to be, 'She's deadly, she's beautiful!'

During the walk to the turtle farm, we talked about mangrove-tree oysters, catching crabs, and other subjects with which I was familiar. They told me how women used to scrape poisonous red wood into pools of water. This would kill the fish, which would float to the surface and then be easily harvested. The children who had tagged along with us were warned about stone fish, which are poisonous shells that look like fish. During our return, Linda and Clara carried the smallest children on their backs. We ended a very pleasant walk by making plans to go fishing the following afternoon.

When I arrived at the appointed time of two o'clock, Clara and Linda were organized to go. As I had suggested, I had brought tins of fruit juice; Flora had decided to go with us or rather take us, as she was the only woman on the island who owned her own boat. It even had Flora's name painted on its bow. Flora had markedly reddish, curly hair, and a perpetual scowl on her face (as did so many of the Kaiadilt women). She rowed her boat to the reef area while we three other women and one small niece of Linda's walked. From under rocks, we collected tiny soft crabs to be used as bait. When we started fishing from Flora's boat over the reef, we had all the equipment aboard we needed: nylon hand lines, sinkers, right-sized hooks, bait, knives, and a bucket. Quite a contrast to the disorganized fishing expedition I had gone on three years previously!

I managed to catch the first fish, a fairly small one. Fortunately, I was quite accustomed to taking fish off hooks, handling bait, and sitting in a small, cramped boat. It was important to me to fit in easily with these women, and to feel accepted by them; and I believe I was. My concern was accentuated both by the fact that I had had difficulty getting them to relate to me during my previous visit, and by the realization that until very recently, the Kaiadilt had had no friendly contact with any

Kaiadilt women gathering shrimp for bait

people other than their own tribe.

But to get back to the fishing; Clara and Flora caught many fish, Linda none, and I was successful in pulling in a second one, a beauty weighting about two pounds. We had used all our original bait, so I offered my first tiny fish as bait.

All during this time the three-year-old girl had sat quietly, but involved. Later in the afternoon after school, Clara's five-year-old and two other girls appeared on the beach. So we rowed in to the shore to pick them up and to collect more bait. I viewed four children and four adults in the same 4-metre boat with some apprehension. However, when any child showed signs of becoming fidgety, a quiet, firm admonition from one of the women calmed the restlessness. The ease with which these women maintained order with the children was notable.

It was a very pleasant afternoon. While Clara and I were rowing the boat back to the Kaiadilt area, I decided to offer my one fish to Linda since she had not caught any. Later she insisted that I keep my fish since Clara and Flora had given her some of their catch; so Linda and her family had something to eat other than tea and damper before going off to the movies at seven that evening.

Linda: aged thirty-three
'The Mission saved our lives.'

Linda, of the fishing trip, was one of the three unmarried women discussed in the report of my first trip to the island. Except for the turtle farm visit, I was able to spend little time with Winnie, whom I had also interviewed in 1970. She was involved with the idea of going back to Bentinck, and had written a letter to the Queensland Government concerning this. The third, Cathy, had married the Kaiadilt man to whom she had been 'engaged'. She appeared to be bouncy, happy, and pleased with herself.

In 1973, Linda was working as an assistant to a Queensland Health Department Sanitarian, who was conducting a survey of the incidence of hookworm disease on Mornington.[18] I observed that Linda was obviously organized in her record keeping. The two of us managed to spend some time chatting together, especially discussing the proposed incorporation of the village. Linda minced no words in expressing her opinion, 'Mornington Islanders are stupid. We Bentincks are going to have to go someplace if they take over. The Mission saved our lives. If they (the Mornington Islanders) take over, it will be terrible, there will be fighting, they will do things according to their own laws. It will be harder for Bentincks to get jobs. Most of them do not accept us Bentincks, but there are several who are nice people.'

Linda continued, 'I'm not sure if I'd like to go back to Bentinck permanently, or just for a holiday. If the Government gave us some money, we could use it as a loan and pay it back eventually. We could sell fish, crabs and dugong.[19] We would need refrigeration to send it to Burketown or Sweers Island. There is talk of some company planning to pipe bauxite to Sweers and then load it on big boats from there. That could really help us, if we return to Bentinck.'

Linda finally decided that the only way incorporation could work out, would be to have some very experienced white man run Mornington.

Notes

1. John Cawte, *Brutal Nations,* op. cit. p. 11.
2. Norman B. Tindale, 'Some Population Changes Among the Kaiadilt People of Bentinck Island, Queensland', *Records of the South Australian Museum,* 14, 1962, pp. 297-336.
3. Tindale, ibid., p. 315.
4. Cawte, op. cit., p. 164.
5. R. T. Simmons, Norman B. Tindale, and Joseph B. Birdsell, 'A Blood Group Genetical Survey in Australian Aborigines of Bentinck, Mornington and Forsyth Islands, Gulf of Carpentaria', *American Journal of Physical Anthropology* 20, 1962, p. 319. The people of Bentinck are unique in possessing no blood group A, and have the highest group B and the highest $R°$ found in Australian Aborigines. The Lardil possess low A, no B, high R^2, low $R°$ and the gene R^z.
6. ibid., pp. 303-320.
7. Tindale, op. cit. pp. 307-308.
8. Cawte, op. cit., p. 16.
9. The middle-aged Kaiadilt women not infrequently have continued to make cuts on their bodies with sharp objects when they were sad or sick. After this self-mutilation they reported that they felt better. The Kaiadilt term for this is *njiltanjilt* and is similar to the Lardil *nurri-nurri,* see p. 92. This practice is unrelated to the Aboriginal custom of inducing cicatrices for decorative purposes.
10. Tindale, op. cit., pp. 319-336. Tindale produced a classificatory record of the Kaiadilt according to their horde *(dolnoro),* sex, and approximate age. The Kaiadilt mentioned in the text of this chapter are not called by their actual names. However, the pseudonyms used are listed below with the classificatory designation given by Tindale.
    Olly: X F. 15.
    Lena: W f. 6.
    Lena's father: W. 3.
    Lena's mother: V f. 4.
    Old Jack: V. 3.
    Winnie: Y f. 4.
    Cathy: X F. 18.
    Linda: W f. 9.
    Carrie: T f. 13.
    Clara: Y f. 3.
    Clara's father: Y. 2.
    Clara's mother: S f. 14.
    Flora: S f. 24.
11. In 1941, Olly, her husband, and three children were sent from Allen Island to

Aurukun, a Mission several hundred miles north on the York Peninsula, by Burketown police after her husband's involvement in a murder. He died at Aurukun. Subsequently Olly had two additional children, each fathered by different men. Olly and her children were sent to Mornington in 1953 to join the other Bentincks.

12. Apparently the taboo of the Lardil of having no man present at a birth was not practised by the Kaiadilt.

13. These four men would probably all have been considered cousin-brothers, and not available as mates according to kinship. However, this was never mentioned by the women.

14. It was typical of the Islanders to respond in such a passive-aggressive fashion in order to avoid complying with external demands, rather than to admit openly an objection or an inability. It was in such a manner that Elsie's nephew had reacted to her request for repair of her shower door.

15. This generalization was endorsed by some of the Mission staff.

16. Simmons, et. al., op. cit., p. 318.

17. At that time I had not been aware that there had been no dingoes on Bentinck, so perhaps owning a dog was still not a part of their culture. However, there was a tone to Linda's comment that appeared to reveal envy and resentment that only the Lardil apparently had been financially able to import a dog.

18. Only one case of hookworm was found in the sample of people studied.

19. It was illegal for anyone to kill dugong except Aborigines and then only for their own use.

13
Reflections

In reflecting about the content of the biographical material, it is most striking that these women truly represent transitional figures. This is shown both by their individual personalities and by the society in which they live, reflecting both their traditional heritage and their Westernization. The two disparate cultural streams run parallel through the lives of the women without their apparent awareness of the incongruities. Most tend to be equally comfortable with sorcery, magic, and other ancestral beliefs and with various Western practices, ideas, and ideals to which they have been exposed.

Most are no longer subservient to their husbands in their personal and community lives. They have negotiated the early authoritarian restrictions of the original Mission and its attitude toward sexual matters. Their current, more permissive, attitude towards sexual behaviour no doubt reveals aspects of the practices from the pre-Mission days and those developing in modern day Western society; and even in the brief period of three years, the women had become more accepting of contraceptive measures.

In fifty years or less they had made the transition from a polygamous family style to a monogamous one. However, the latter type of nuclear family and marriage is showing signs of dissolution with a number of factors contributing to this. Kinship, important in choosing marriage partners and in many social obligations, although weakened both by the Mission and other Western influences, continues to partly influence the lives of the Mornington islanders. They are attempting to rekindle their Aboriginal heritage by renewed interest in kinship and other traditional practices and beliefs. At the same time, they wish for the comforts and opportunities of Western society and must take over the responsibility of running their own community. Thus, the lives of the Aboriginal women on Mornington Island are in a transitional state.

Discordant Beliefs

There is a discordance between the beliefs and practices inherited from their ancestors and those adopted from their contact with Western culture which influence their lives. Apparently these contradictions have aroused little or no overt anxiety or defensiveness. These observations are supported by Cawte in his study of the island inhabitants. Cawte used four parameters to measure culture identity: acquisition of Western culture, emulation of Western culture, retention of traditional activities, and retention of traditional beliefs. His findings led him to conclude that neither acquisition nor emulation of Western ways had displaced the ancestral tribal beliefs. He further found that neither acquisition of Western culture nor retention of traditional activities was correlated with psychological disability or mental illness.

It is often reported that peoples who have been converted to Christianity by missionaries maintain most of their pagan beliefs under a facade of Christian persuasion.[2] As Winter said,[3] the adoption of new beliefs is a relatively easy task; however, the extinction of the old ones is difficult. Psychological conflict from the two belief systems is more likely to arise in individuals if conversion to Christianity takes place when they are adults.

The middle-aged Lardil, however, were removed from their tribal families at a relatively early age and spent most of their developing years under the authoritarian control and Christian teachings of the Mission. As Elsie and the others have reported, it was not until they became adults that they developed curiosity about their traditional culture, and then had to relearn much of it from the surviving elders. It is, therefore, interesting that they then embraced traditional beliefs in an uncritical manner, suggesting that their original cultural identity persisted beneath a veneer of Christianity.

The ability of Elsie and others to tolerate dual, and at times disparate, belief systems would seem to conflict with the theory of cognitive dissonance as formulated by Festinger.[4] He asserted that there is always pressure for an individual to reduce inconsistencies in thinking. However, as he pointed out, the social group is a major vehicle for either reducing or maintaining dissonant beliefs. Among the Lardil, where many share the seeming dissonant concepts, the pressure for reduction of the incongruities is markedly lessened by the social support of the group. In fact, most appear not to perceive the inconsistencies in the beliefs drawn from the two cultures that inform their lives.

Individuals maintain certain incompatible wishes and ideas.

However, most tend to justify them by rationalization or by the use of other ego defense mechanisms. However, if these manoeuvres, usually unconscious, are not successful in dealing with the incongruities, overt anxiety or other psychological symptoms are experienced. The apparent absence of overt anxiety among the Lardil with respect to cognitive dissonance, therefore, leads one to wonder about the possible defenses employed to maintain incompatible beliefs. The social sanctions of the community may be sufficient for the maintenance of their discordant beliefs.

Possible Explanations for Continuation of Some of the Traditional Beliefs

Sorcery. The examples given by the women, in which sorcery was implicated as the possible cause of illness, death, or madness, occurred after the fact, that is retrospectively. As I heard the various tales, it seemed that when a person becomes ill he worries about whom he may have wronged, who in turn would employ sorcery in retaliation. This worry would seem to imply guilt over some actual or imagined misdeed or evil wish. However, instead of feeling the guilt as such, the person who becomes sick would blame someone else for inflicting illness on him by the use of *puri-puri.* Currently, the Lardil tend to think of the sorcerer as some Aborigine on the mainland, so that the evil doer is even more distant and impersonal.

A psychodynamic formulation would be that the guilt is unconscious, and is guarded against by the defense mechanisms of displacement and projection; the blame is placed on an unnamed or unknown person.

It is of note that the individual who was most verbal and adamant concerning the subject of sorcery was one who perhaps had the most immediate reason for guilt feelings. Another denied any awareness of guilt and expressed disbelief in sorcery. A third woman, who displayed discomfort when discussing the subject; rationalized sorcery as possibly being one of the strange ways in which God acts. The concept of sorcery is probably cognitively dissonant for her; thus she tried to reduce the incongruity.

Because sorcery is part of the cultural belief, it offers a plausible explanation for the unknown and feared, that is, illness and death. A different explanation for the belief in sorcery as maintained by the Lardil was offered by Cawte,[5] who has been the only person to report a study of this belief as held by this group of Aborigines. He postulated that it is a form of social, peer group control. In other words, one complies with the moral-legal code of his society, or risks becoming accused of sorcery and having to endure a climate of adverse social opinion. Cawte also pointed out that the complaint of sorcery arises *ex post facto,* and that the role of the victim is more important than that of the sorcerer. Combining the two hypotheses, we can conclude that sorcery as perceived by the Lardil serves a variety of psycho-social functions.

Malgri

As was so vividly described by several of the women, *malgri* results from having the smell of land food on one's hands when one goes into the sea. Unless all traces of the odour of land foods are removed by washing them away, a totem of that locality, in the form of an evil spirit in the sea, such as the rainbow serpent, will enter the offending individual. The victim then develops abdominal cramps and swelling, marked constipation, and sometimes vomiting. Currently some go to the nursing sisters for treatment. However, the services of a tribal songman are usually considered more effective.

Cawte regarded *malgri* as specific to the Lardil culture and offered a number of possible explanations to account for this 'spirit intrusion' syndrome.[6] The genesis of the syndrome lies in the pre-village past. Before the movement of all the people to the village area, the land was divided into estates and the adjacent sea coast divided into geographic areas called littorals. Thus, each family grouping had its own estate and littoral and totem guardian spirit. According to Gully Peters, if one went into the sea area of his own littoral he would not get *malgri* as the totem spirit of the area recognized the smell of the person. However, if one went into the sea belonging to another family grouping, the spirit totem would fail to recognize his body odour and would attack (enter) him as a trespasser or poacher. In this way, the fear of *malgri* acted as a means of social-legal control to maintain territoriality.

Now that all the islanders have forsaken their family littorals, one needs to wonder what function the perpetuation of the belief in this intrusion syndrome serves. I shall offer an explanation from my own ethnocentric bias. The fear of *malgri* is phobic in nature and if the phobic situation is not avoided, anxiety or hysteroid-like symptoms result. The *malgri* symptoms are removed by the blowing and chanting of a songman, whose technique resembles a hypnotic procedure.

Phobic objects and situations are symbolic displacements of anxiety resulting from unconscious intra-psychic conflict. Phobic type of fear is often reinforced by the immediate society, as is the case with *malgri*. It is not possible to know what might have been the conflict in the *malgri* victims who were described to me. However, all the attacks that were reported occurred in children, except for Elsie's story of Adam. In these children the most likely source of conflict would have been over rebellious impulses against their parents. They then disobeyed parental injunctions by not removing land smells before going swimming and developed the syndrome. However, their rebellious impulses (or misdeeds) were symbolically forgiven by the revered songman, a powerful parent substitute. Explained in these psychodynamic terms, a belief that originally developed as a means of territorial control of a social-legal nature, has become a psychosocial phenomenon serving a different purpose. The phobic fear of *malgri* continues to exercise a type of control.

Magic and the Power of Suggestion. Elsie's dream following her mother's death, in which a bright light was reflected from a tin can back to her mother's grave, offers an example of the fear of 'spirit intrusion' from the dead. However, this story had a happy ending. In her dream her dead mother gave a magic stone to her favourite nephew that, according to Elsie, still endows him with the ability to cure.

In fact, most of Elsie's stories of magic were of a curative nature, rather than destructive. Other practices were conducive to health. She believed in them, although the cure (or improvement) might be only temporary. Even my neurological examination was perceived by her as giving temporary relief to her back and leg discomfort. The power of suggestion was obviously a strong influence for Elsie as for most of the Lardil. The songmen (or medicine men) knew the power of faith and its influence, which can be exercised by the mind over the body. They worked psychologically to get rid of the animistic causes of illness.[7] Elsie and others continue the magical rituals and native remedies but just as readily turn to Western medicine for help; again, an example of how these women operate under the influence of their two cognitive worlds.

Kinship

Throughout the material that has been presented are many references to kinship practices as these applied to marriage customs and to various social taboos and obligations. Complex kinship rules determining acceptable marriage partners as well as other social mores had been highly developed by the many Aboriginal groups over many years. An elaborate eight subsection kinship system, apparently copied from Aboriginal groups on the nearby Mainland, had been relatively late in becoming a part of the tradition of the pre-Mission Lardil. In Chapter 2, Dick Roughsey's lengthy description of the Lardil kinship practices is recorded. However, Gully Peters expressed it succinctly by saying, 'In the old days some of the marriages were right-head and some were wrong.'

When the approved kinship rules were applied, there should have been no dispute as to who should marry whom, as a girl child would be 'promised' at birth to an older male. By regulating to whom a woman could speak or a man could touch, incest and other sexual taboos could be avoided. Magico-spiritual practices were pre-ordained by the designation of the uncle (mother's brother) and others who were responsible for the circumcision rites and other initiation practices that were so important in the passage of a boy into manhood.

The kinship obligations carried over into many aspects of their extended family. The roles of the elders, the men, and the women, and the children were well defined. The elders would care for the young children, while the men went hunting and the women gathered reef and land foods. At the same time they taught the growing children these skills. The bounty would be shared with the kinship group less fortunate in their gathering and hunting. It followed that the elders would always be provided for.

When reflecting upon the lives of the various women, it is evident that while the subject of kinship was part of their thinking, it was not an intimate part of their everyday lives. None of the older or younger Lardil women who are described in this book reported being married according to the traditional kinship rules. Only Elsie's and Dick's union is 'almost right-head'. No doubt the Mission marriage arrangements account in part for some of this. At least one (Ethel Tunney) reported that she refused to marry the man to whom she had been 'promised'. None professed to have promised any of their children so as to promote a 'right-head' marriage. They thought it preferable to allow their children to make a free choice of a mate. Their stated preference for sons-in-law was for hard-working, non-drinking men.

Contradicting this was the occasional mention of fights that have broken out between families if a wrong-head marriage was contemplated. While there was evidence of yearning for more regulation of marriage along the lines that would promote their cultured heritage, there would seem to be no turning back to this. Some of the informants seemed to imagine that return to such old customs would solve some of their problems, but none seemed to really believe this, and they were aware it would not be acceptable to the younger generation.

Social taboos and obligations that should be shown to one's kin group reflected inconsistencies and lack of compliance. While the designations of father, uncle, cousin, and other terms are still used in the traditional manner, prohibitions such as not speaking directly to a brother, were disregarded. Pearl hinted that she missed having her own kinship group available to her during her developing years, but claimed to feel completely accepted by her husband's extended family. Rose Johns blamed many of her troubles on being an outsider and having no kin to help her. Others, shunned by their mothers-in-law, failed to mention that violation of kinship regulations had anything to do with the hostility they experienced.

In the earlier days, members of a kinship group could expect relatives to share food and possessions as well as perform favours. There were a number or examples where relatives no longer complied with this practice, or if they did, they expected rewards. It was evident that Elsie considered that this custom should be in operation. This type of obligation has no doubt been diluted by the influence of Western culture, where currency is the mode of exchange, and perhaps reflects resentment when demands and expectations of help are considered excessive. It is implicit that some women wish for strengthening of the kinship bonds so that they could expect more attention and support from their offspring as they grow older. As we shall see, this is particularly true of the Kaiadilt, although kinship in the usual Aboriginal context was never as potent an influence for this group.

In ways, kinship rules and obligations for the mutual support of an extended family sound desirable; however, it is dubious that the adoption of Western ways will promote this.

Aspects of Their Sexual Lives
In group discussions, some of the middle-aged women displayed discomfort in speaking of sexual matters. However, when they talked with me individually they were relatively open and free in discussing their sexual life.

The strict controls and warnings concerning sexuality given by the missionaries to these dormitory-reared girls did not necessarily produce the attitude that sex is an evil, sinful interest or activity. From their descriptions, some foreplay may be a part of the sexual act. Pleasure was reported by a number of the women, who were inclined to see intercourse as both a duty and a pleasure. However, several of the women had found the sexual act less than a satisfying experience. Not only were they usually frigid, they even had unpleasant emotional or physical responses, which they tended to conceal from their husbands.

In women everywhere psychosexual development and response to adult sexuality are complex and highly variable. From the material elicited from the Lardil group (more specifically the older ones), I was not able to detect any aspects that could be considered unique to them. There was repression of memories concerning pre-dormitory development. Except in the instances when the couple chose each other, marriages occurred as a result of the instigation of the 'missionary-father'. Since arranged marriages were part of the Aboriginal kinship tradition, there was little evidence of resentment of this practice. The women spoke of the missionary in residence during their school years with obvious warmth and fondness.

Yet, these now middle-aged women remembered responding as brides to their new husbands with anxiety as to a stranger. Probably the positive feelings for the missionary assisted the eventual development of a reasonable marital relationship, men being perceived in this model as not unduly threatening even though initially unfamiliar.

It is tempting to speculate about possible factors contributing to Elsie's difficulty in sexual gratification. She denied any knowledge about sex until after she left the dormitory. She remembered her father as having deserted her mother, although this is in contrast to other information supplied to me. Her description of her father's fighting ability made him appear as if he were a hero in her eyes. She portrayed him as a man who 'ran' after many women and finally settled down to live with 'Old Kate'. It was with her father and Old Kate that Elsie remembered spending most of her time during the two years that the dormitory was closed during World War II. It is suggested that in fantasy she invested her father's aggressive and sexual prowess with heroic properties, while at the same time she was influenced by Mission teachings that men were to be avoided and sex was a taboo subject. It is as if an unresolved oedipal attachment, with its attendant guilt accentuated by the Mission admonitions, may account for her lack of libidinal satisfaction.

During the early married life the former 'dormitory girls' had no method available to prevent conception, so that most have borne from six to ten children. They denied any knowledge of tribal lore for the induction of abortion. Elsie apparently had perceived the rudiments of the so-called rhythm system of contraception, possibly as a result of her European contacts, and later she sought the pill. Most of the women had not requested contraception, either because they were not aware of its availability or for more subjective reasons. Several of the women had wished for such a measure, but because of shyness or passivity could not ask. They readily accepted the intrauterine coil when recommended by the flying-doctor.

Quality of Mothering

The quality of mothering ranged widely among these Aboriginal women. There were those whose child-rearing philosophy was revealed by such wise statements as 'if you don't respect your children, they won't respect you', and 'there is a time to love them and a time to be hard with them'. In contrast, Elsie and many other mothers were deeply concerned about, but confused by, their offspring. They found discipline and control difficult.

Some of the factors that contributed to the difficulties these mothers experienced are evident. Notable is the rapid transition in their way of life, from their polygynous tribal beginnings to the unique dormitory rearing, and then to marriage in a Western-type family structure. They had no prototype for the job of being parents in a settled family situation.

The Lardil women in their child-rearing practices showed again both the traditional and the Western influences. Most told of regular breast-feeding, while Elsie and others described their nursing habits to be more in the nature of a pacifier, that is, giving them 'a suck to make them quiet'. Currently, weaning takes place about age one, with the breast milk previously having been supplemented with appropriate soft foods.

Without exception, the women questioned reported very early bowel training, starting when the baby is six to twelve months old. In connection with the subject of bowel training, one recalls Pearl Yates's statement, 'If they learn to be tidy when young, they will be tidy when they grow up.' This is contrary to the permissive attitude reported by Cawte.[8] However, it appeared that frequently this 'training' consisted of running after the young child with a pottie when the mothers observed defecatory body movement, rather than the child asking for the pottie.

In other areas, the parents were permissive, and the children led unregulated lives as was characteristic of the customs in the pre-Mission days. After infancy, food was given on demand and there was a marked lack of regulation of mealtime and bedtime. Children, even the small ones, wandered about as they wished with little or no evidence of supervision from adults. However, there was a great deal of body contact between parents and small children, as well as between older and younger children. At unexpected moments harsh and punitive actions tended to erupt through the permissiveness. A generally tolerated activity might elicit rage, depending on the parent's mood at the time.

While many of the mothers expressed the wish for their children to have a better education and better chance in life than they, they showed little interest in school performance and little inclination to communicate with the teachers. Tardiness or failure to attend school did not appear to be a cause for concern.

Some of the mothers had set limits and had expectations of performance of tasks, as exemplified by Pearl Yates. Others so constantly warned their offspring of potential dangers that they become constricted in their behaviour, as shown by the interaction of Mrs Vines and her daughter. However, more often, mothers like Elsie growled and fussed and threatened, but failed to follow through with suitable action, with the result that their children quickly learned that talk was meaningless. Confrontation was avoided, even when unacceptable activity was obvious. This was well illustrated by Elsie's failure to challenge her sons when money was missing from her purse.

This lack of confrontation and control of offspring was in direct contrast to what the middle-aged parents experienced in the dormitory. Perhaps it reflected attitudes from pre-Mission times. As reported to me, in the old days if parents severely punished a child, the grandparents or other relatives might take the child away. Elsie said, 'Children are more spoiled now than when we lived in the Mission: it's the softness of the parents.' Yet she also reported that her father told her, 'Don't hit children, be kind to them'. In these two statements, Elsie revealed the disparate parental models that she experienced. Neither model was sufficiently internalized to allow her to be without conflict in her role as mother.

Many mothers wished that there could be something like the dormitory to take the responsibility for disciplining their children and for indoctrinating them into a more responsible and productive way of life as they approach adulthood. They decried the disinclination of many of their husbands to help with discipline. They had ambitions and ideals for their progeny, but were baffled as to how to help or motivate them toward these goals.

The Younger Lardil Women
The younger women, those under thirty, were a more heterogeneous group than those reared in the dormitory. The younger women were less inclined to continue some of the traditional practices. They tended to be vague about the subject of whether or not their marriage was righthead. This was confirmed by Cawte's study of cultural identity, which also showed higher acquisition of Western traits in those under thirty-five years of age.[9]

The younger women presented greater differences in their personalities than the middle-aged group: some were open and verbal; others were elusive, and apparently unable to cross the cultural gap in order to be free in an interview situation. In their daily lives some were hard-working and reliable; others exhibited immature behaviour, and were not motivated to do much of anything that might be considered constructive. Some were dissatisfied with their life situation, but were unable to take realistic steps to improve it.

Current Transitional Trends in the Family Unit. A number of the younger women had several children and no husband. Most of the younger unmarried women expressed marked interest in having husbands and nice homes. However, their desires will be difficult to fulfil. There are a number of factors contributing to this, including the ambivalent attitudes of their mothers.

Most mothers expressed the wish that their daughters would marry hard-working, non-drinking men. They deplored the lack of initiative and the disinclination to work displayed by many of the younger Lardil men. They were frightened by the increased fighting among the men since the legalization of beer. The older women despair of their daughters finding husbands who would meet with their approval.

Currently, the babies of the younger women who do not marry are readily accepted by the grandparents. If a young woman is impregnated while working or visiting on the mainland, the pregnancy may be more acceptable since the father of the baby is unknown. In this situation the grandparents have no preformed antipathy to him and his family.

However, frequently there is marked hostility between families when a young woman is impregnated by a young man on the island, and pressure is exerted by the relatives for them not to marry. While the traditional practice of promising a child to promote a right-head marriage is infrequent now, the objection to marriage often reflects the fact that it would not be according to the kinship rules. Another objection can be based on the idea that the parents know too many 'bad things' about the prospective bride or groom and their families. Therefore, often there is great opposition to a proposed marriage of a young couple. While discussing this with an elder woman, looked upon by the islanders as a wise grandmother, she said, 'If I say to the parents why not *let* them marry,' this may be interpreted as 'you want us to *force* them to marry'.

About 10 per cent of the younger children have had white fathers. This evidence of miscegenation does not evoke criticism from the grandmothers, in spite of the expressed wish of many of the older women for their daughters not to cohabit with white men, and not give them half-caste grandchildren.

There are other elements contributing to the disinclination of the young adults to marry and set up their own nuclear families.[10] The Western-style family was imposed on only one generation; that is, those reared in the Mission dormitory. The present day Mission does not exert the authoritarian influence that the original Mission did. In the absence of such authority, one generation is probably not long enough for this type of cultural change to become self-perpetuating in this society.

The paucity of social and economic stimulation has been conducive to passivity and lack of initiative in the young male. There is little motivation or ostensible reward for taking on the responsibility of a wife and children. The shared affection and emotional support and satisfaction in a marriage is apparently not evident to these young men.

The offspring of the young women are absorbed into their own parents' household and the government money from child endowment provides for the meagre necessities. What type of parental figures these young children, especially the boys, will have is problematical. The grandfathers are ageing, and the responsibility of the uncle (mother's brother) for introducing the boy into the rites of passage into manhood has long disappeared with the abolition of the initiation-circumcision ceremonies that were so important in the pre-Mission tribal culture.

As reported previously, there appears to be more concern about drinking and gambling than about sexual promiscuity. Some have forsaken their legal spouses to live with others. These, and more transient extra-marital affairs, can create a lot of dissension and gossip at the time they occur. But soon the hostilities and talk die down; there is little or no evidence of rejection, or ostracism of the persons concerned from the group, even by the immediate kinship family. This ready acceptance may reflect the sexual practices of the pre-Mission days, when wife-swapping or wife-lending was fairly common. The sexual mores then were quite different from those introduced by the white Christian ethic.

The current disruption of the nuclear family has particularly serious implications for the socialization of the children, and perhaps for the structure of the family in future generations.

Attitudes Toward Birth Control.

The younger women show the potential of having as many children as did their mothers. The birth rate in 1970 was 4 to 5 per cent: this is in contrast to a less than 2 per cent birth rate among Australians of European ancestry. Over half of the island population is under twenty years of age.

While there were no religious contra-indications, in 1970 the Mission staff had not attempted to educate the people concerning family planning. The nursing sisters, who usually come to the Mission for a two-year period, had found the women to be unreliable 'pill' takers. A few of the women who had had five or six pregnancies, and who were showing signs of physical debility as the result of repeated or frequent child bearing or both, had been fitted with an intrauterine device by the flying-doctor. In 1973, the hospital records showed thirty-four women had been so fitted, while six were taking oral contraceptives. This number included the women who had refused to discuss contraception with me during my earlier visit, apparently because they were too 'shy'. Giving contraceptives to the unmarried had not been considered in 1970. In the intervening three years, two girls who had borne babies at the age of fourteen had been fitted with an intrauterine coil, with the permission of their parents.

The women had apparently become more accepting of contraception. Their motivation for accepting change in personal practices is reflected in this. Perhaps the Islanders may be receptive to education in family planning, even though it is not one of their social concepts. Without such education, the residents of the island are too isolated to have any appreciation or concern about over-population, and additional babies are supported by child endowment.

How young husbands would accept the idea of drastically limiting family size in unknown. There was some evidence that husbands and wives have difficulty discussing sexual matters, and also that 'husbands may feel their wives are resisting them if they do not have babies'. As near as could be ascertained the traditional Aboriginal concept that impregnation resulted from a spirit-child entering the womb was no longer held by these women.[11]

It will be in large part the responsibility of these younger women (and men) to promote the success or failure of the village incorporation. They show less uniformity than their parents in their ideas, work habits, and initiative. It is in this younger age group that drinking and gambling are more prevalent. The men in this age group, although not studied in detail, seem as variable in their work habits and sense of responsibility as are the young women. It is the young men who show a disinclination for marriage. One must ask the question, if given the responsibility for the management of the island and their lives, how will the younger people respond to this change? Will it increase their sense of purpose and self-esteem?

The Kaiadilt Women

It is evident that in the short period of twenty-five years, the younger Kaiadilt women have changed from a palaeolithic lifestyle to having embraced some of the accoutrements of Western society. This is exemplified by their language, their ability to verbalize, their ideas, their dress, and the addition of new foods to their diet.

The middle-aged women continued to appear emaciated and dishevelled. They wanted to converse with me, but because of the language barrier this was difficult. Apparently, they did not perceive the social distance that made it difficult initially for the younger women to relate to me.

The younger Kaiadilt women were acutely aware of being socially ostracized by the majority of the Lardil; also, they were not as accustomed to associating with white people as were most of the Lardil. During my second visit to the island, after I made contact through Clara, these younger Kaiadilt women seemed to welcome relating to me, and I felt accepted by them.

The Kaiadilt women were no longer being 'bossed' by the men. In fact, because of the scarcity of men, they were now running their meagre households. Clara was able to afford to have a more 'proper' house built for her, and Flora owned her own boat. When we went fishing, they were well-organized. In contrast to the Lardil, they have more recently needed to rely on their own resources or die. Although they now receive the same allotments as the Lardil, they have not had as long a history of dependency. They do not have as large a kin or tribal grouping on which to rely. These factors may contribute to their being better organized in a native pursuit such as fishing, and to being more inclined to report for menial jobs.

It had been reported that the Kaiadilt do not look after their old and their sick. This was especially true when they first arrived on the island. However, there is evidence to the contrary, as was demonstrated by Carrie's concern for the elderly. The firm but kind way they dealt with the children was notable. These children, a number of whom were part-white, were vigorous and friendly, engaging in manner, and appeared well-fed. This was in contrast to their grandmothers.

Marriage in the Western tradition has been difficult for them to follow. In part, this is based on the reality that there are eleven unmarried women and only four men of marriageable age. They made no mention that kinship rules would prevent marriage. There appeared to be even more pressure against marriage from the older Kaiadilt women than from the Lardil. If a youth does marry, the daughter-in-law or son-in-law may be shunned. Most of the young adults appear to accept the role their mothers have cast them in, that is, that of provider of meagre income from the limited employment available and from the various government allotments.

The Kaiadilt want to maintain cohesion in their group for their own security. Most remember something of their desperate situation while living on Bentinck; they are grateful to the Mission for rescuing them.

The socio-cultural exclusion that the Kaiadilt have experienced in relation to the dominant Lardil has put them in a marginal situation.[12] They show certain of the psychological traits associated with this type of situation, especially feelings of uncertainty and of rejection. According to the findings of Cawte,[13] they suffer more emotional and physical distress than do the Lardil. In his cultural identity studies, they scored lowest in the acquisition and emulation of Western culture, and had the highest scores on retention of traditional activities and beliefs. As would be expected, as a group, they have more difficulty in facing a divergent culture. While initially, as a result of their extreme social and environmental decline, the Kaiadilt were perceived by many of the Lardil as barely human, they certainly cannot be so regarded today.[14]

The Kaiadilt feel the threat of the Mission withdrawal so strongly that they fear they may be forced to leave Mornington. This, in part, was the stimulus for a small group (nine Kaiadilt and two Lardil) to return to Bentinck in an attempt to resettle the Island. They were transported by a boat owned by one of the white workers, the man developing the turtle farm. The Lardil couple had a small boat with an outboard motor to allow for return to Mornington in case of illness or other difficulties. During a three-month period, while living in tents, they were able to plant a garden and clear a small airstrip. They obtained much of their food from the land and the sea as in former times. They made handcrafts to help finance their venture. (Some of this information was supplied by Mr Donald MacLeod, the white man helping them.)

A letter had been written to the Queensland Government by one of the young Kaiadilt women asking for permission to resettle their native island. They had even discussed the possibility of a commercial seafood venture if the neighbouring Sweers Island becomes a deep-sea port for shipping bauxite.

After having been rescued 'from the edge of annihilation' by the Mission, they fear what the future on Mornington Island holds for them. Could they return to Bentinck Island and become self-sufficient? How much of their recently deserted life-style would or could they resume? Might they be able to develop a commercial seafood operation? Their idea of returning to Bentinck Island in many ways may be unrealistic; however, they are capable of conceiving some alternatives for their future.

Current Status of the Women

Over the years the role or status of the Aboriginal woman has been considered by research workers to be much inferior to that of the man. Such words as 'chattel' or 'pawn' have been applied to her. Most male writers, presumably with male informants, have tended to see the Aboriginal women as having an inferior role. A few researchers,[15] who worked primarily with women informants, have reported a more equal relationship between the sexes. As a woman researcher, who spoke mainly with women, I may have the same bias as others of my own sex.

The majority of the Lardil women considered their husbands to be the boss in the family. However, many women not only run the household affairs, they are active in decision-making, and may take the role of leader. Others resent the demands or dependency of their husbands.

White stated, 'Aboriginal women are partners rather than pawns or chattels of men.'[16] She qualified this by saying, 'Their status is everywhere that of junior partner, and women accept this role.' However, White based her conclusions on the traditional Aboriginal culture in which the man claimed the sole power to create spiritual life, arranged betrothals, and had more right to sexual freedom.

Within the present-day Mornington group of Aborigines several opposing forces have promoted more equalization of the roles of women and men. With the adoption of Christian practices, the importance of men in the spiritual life has diminished. While men are the church elders, only a few attend services or take any active part in policy-making. Several of the older men do offer prayers, read the scriptures, and about once a month deliver a sermon. In contrast, a greater number of women regularly attend services and provide the choir music, and are active in the Womens Group. This has regular meetings for Bible study and promotes social and fund-raising activities. The women are currently the 'backbone' of the local church.

With the marriages for many having been, in part, arranged from the dormitory, there is little disparity in the ages of the marriage partners. When polygyny was practiced, frequently a girl child was promised to a man many years older than she. This facilitated male dominance.

While the opportunity for women to earn cash income is somewhat less than for men, they have gained some degree of financial control through the various allotments available to them. As a result of the recently created Supporting Mothers Benefit, the financial need for a supporting husband has been lessened.

The women now rarely collect bush foods, so that their daily lives centre around domestic chores and caring for the children. There is time for frequent trips to the village store, for attending church activities, and for socializing. The women do not miss the old way of life. It was cold and damp in the bush during the wet season. Those that have the new conveniences such as running water, refrigeration, and electricity are pleased. Some even find it more comfortable to sit on chairs, rather than to continue the more customary manner of sitting on the floor or ground.

As stated previously, job opportunities are more limited for women; however, a few hold such 'white-collar' positions as teachers assistants, nursing aides, and office workers. They are gaining some political power by being elected to the village Council and appointed to the

Board of Directors of the proposed Incorporation. They like the change in their status. They have adjusted to it and there is no tendency for backward mobility, that is, for becoming a pawn.

Notes

1. John Cawte, *Brutal Nations,* op. cit., pp. 84-97.
2. Charles Rowley, *The New Guinea Villager: The Impact of Colonial Rule of Primitive Society and Economy.* New York, Frederick A. Praeger, 1966, p. 150; Edward H. Winter, *Beyond The Mountains of the Moon.* London, Routledge & Kegan Paul, 1959, p. 263.
3. Edward H. Winter, *Beyond the Mountains of the Moon.* London, Routledge & Kegan Paul, 1959, p. 263.
4. Leon Festinger, *A Theory of Cognitive Dissonance.* Stanford, California: Stanford University Press, 1957, p. 192.
5. John Cawte, *Medicine is the Law.* Honolulu, University Press of Hawaii, 1974, pp. 85-105.
6. John Cawte, op. cit., pp. 106-119.
7. A. P. Elkin, *The Australian Aborigines.* Garden City, New York, Doubleday & Co., Inc., 1964, pp. 212-213.
8. John Cawte, *Cruel, Poor and Brutal Nations,* op. cit. p. 103.
9. ibid., p. 90.
10. Virginia Huffer, 'Australian Aborigine: Transition in Family Grouping', *Family Process* 12, 1973, pp. 303-315.
11. See Chapter 11, note 1.
12. H. F. Dickie-Clark, *The Marginal Situation.* London, Routledge and Kegan Paul, 1966, pp. 27-48.
13. John Cawte, *Brutal Nations,* op. cit. p. 77, p. 90.
14. Colin M. Turnbull in his book, *The Mountain People,* New York, Simon and Schuster, 1972, vividly portrayed an isolated African tribe, the Ik, as having ceased to be human as a result of overwhelming depletion of their basic resources. Later, John B. Calhoun in an article in *Smithsonian,* 3, 1972, pp. 27-32, compared the Kaiadilt with the Ik, in that both groups had had such extreme individual and social decay. He postulated that their 'dehumanization' might portend a chilling end for mankind, if all resources were destroyed as a result of over-population or other catastrophies.
    In a personal discussion with Turnbull we felt that the former Bentinck Islanders could not have undergone the 'dehumanization' ascribed to the Ik. Never in twenty-five years could one imagine that the Ik could have made the changes that the younger Kaiadilt have made. Anyone who has read Turnbull's book could not imagine an Ik becoming as gracious and poised as Clara, or being as positive in their relations with the children as Linda. Certainly an Ik would never have shared his fish with another as did Clara.
15. Phyllis Kaberry, *Aboriginal Woman, Sacred and Profane.* London, George Routledge and Sons, 1939; Jane Goodale, *Tiwi Wives.* Seattle, University of Washington Press, 1971.
16. Isobel M. White, 'Aboriginal Woman's Status Resolved: A Paradox', in *Woman's Role in Aboriginal Society.* Fay Gale (ed.) Australian Institute of Aboriginal Studies, Canberra 1970, p. 21.

14
The Women
and Psychocultural Adaptation

The preceding chapters have told the life story of Elsie Roughsey as related by her. Biographical facets of some of the other women of Mornington Island have been presented more briefly. Some of my reflections concerning the personal, cultural, and social circumstances of their lives have been given in chapter 13.

The lives of these women remain in a state of psychocultural transition. During the sixty years existence of the Mission Reserve, bringing with it the Protestant Christian ethic, education, and European customs, the women (and men) from childhood on have had to cope with an externally imposed culture. How successful have they been in dealing with these innovations, and what will the future demand of them in view of the proposed withdrawal of the Mission control? Since personality and culture are interactive, it is pertinent to discuss various aspects of psychocultural adaptation as they apply to the women who live on Mornington Island.

The concept of adaptation involves the capacity to cope reasonably, yet advantageously, with the environment.[1] In examining this crucial issue for these Aboriginal women, I shall use both the psychoanalytic perspective, particularly as formulated by Heinz Hartmann,[2] and a complementary anthropological model as developed by George Spindler and others.[3]

Hartmann stated, 'Adaptation is primarily a reciprocal relationship between the organism and his environment . . . Two processes are involved: human action adapts the environment to human function, and then the human being adapts (secondarily) to the environment which he has helped create.'[4] This is in the realm of ego psychology which includes such ego functions as the testing of reality, the regulation and control of instinctual drives, and the maintenance of friendly relations with other individuals over a prolonged period of time. Ego psychology also embraces such processes as learning, making judgments, and planning for the future. The ego functions enable the individual to delay immediate gratification for future gain. Most important in ego psychology is the capacity of the individual personality to feel, think, and act in an organized and directed manner.

Sprindler observed that, under the influence of cultural change, 'the psychological and cultural dimensions are inter-dependent and inseparable'.[5] He contended that psychocultural adaptation is based on the identity of the people involved, and on their ability to establish cognitive control. Both the sense of one's own identity and the cognitive process are important aspects of ego psychology.

Other anthropologists have examined psychocultural adaptation, as it relates to acculturative change. Born reviewed many theories and proposed four modes of adaptation to an acculturative situation: retreatism, reconciliation, innovation, and withdrawal.[6] During the sixty years that the Lardil have been exposed to Christian teachings and to some aspects of Western culture, their adaptation appeared to reflect Born's concept of reconciliation as 'a combination of the traditional and the new; an attempt to "co-exist" or to "strike a happy medium . . ."' Reconciliation is based on a "tendency toward passive acquiescence to, and even by a degree of active co-operation with the acculturative influence", and by the ability to achieve a "new synthesis".'

The Islanders face a new challenge. They are confronted with the prospect of becoming more responsible for themselves through legal incorporation. This will require further adaptation for the increased autonomy and self-determination to an externally imposed situation. This new condition will demand a different level of integration of ego functions for successful coping.

Since adaptation intimately concerns the interrelations of the psychology of the individual (and group to which he belongs) with the environment in which he lives, both factors will be discussed. Elements of adaptation determined by the environment may conveniently be grouped under their economic, social, and political aspects. It is recognized that any conceptual groupings will overlap, as each is related to the other.

The Environment and Adaptation
Economic Factors. The women of Mornington (and to a lesser extent, the men) live on various financial allotments provided by the Australian government. These allotments provide for the basic necessities, and at times for other items such as radios, cameras, and

admission to the movies. This patronage is perceived by many of the women as salary. The Islanders, having a very limited concept of the larger Australian society, have no idea how dependent upon it they are, even for their very existence.

Although there is little opportunity for monetary employment on the island for the women, even such a possibility may be rejected by them. For example, when the development of a bakery was suggested to some of the women by the Mission Manager, it was refused on the basis that 'it would be too much work'.

There is more employment opportunity for the men, but their jobs are also subsidized by the government or the Mission, with the exception of their handcraft and artistic activities. Many of the men are both gifted and skilled as artisans. The women only assist in these activities. However, handcraft and painting are pursued sporadically, depending on the inclination of the men. Since the handcraft shop has been put under the control of the local people, there is reason to think its profitability may decline in the absence of Mission supervision.

Traditionally the men were 'hunters' of the sea: a number still avail themselves of its bounty to supplement the family diet. However, the potential for commercial export of seafoods has not been developed by either the Aborigines or the government. Instead, strangers in trawlers ply these waters for prawn and fish that are sold to mainland and overseas markets. Sometimes these strangers are not even Australian; massive hauls by trawlers from the nations of the north and west Pacific are often taken. To exploit this aspect of their ecology, the islanders would need, at least initially, financial backing as well as leadership.

Tilling of the soil is not part of the life-style of these former hunting-gathering people. Now that an adequate water supply is available, some of the women (and men) are raising a few vegetables and flowers. Some papaw (papaya) trees have been planted. How active the people will be in extending this cultivation to produce more fresh fruits and vegetables is open to question. The men adapt quickly to handling livestock. Since bullocks were introduced they have thrived and run wild: large numbers now roam the island. There is talk of rounding up these animals with the intention of revitalizing a cattle industry.

It is evident that the Islanders have adapted to a subsistence economy based on provision of resources from outside. There is potential for greater utilization of their native skills and of their ecological resources, but it would require more than organization for its realization, and more than outside financial support and supervisory expertise. It would require some reconstruction of the social personality.

Social Aspects. In traditional times each person had his own role. The songman was the healer. The older men passed on the religious beliefs and hunting techniques to the younger men. The women were inferior in the magico-religious practices. Their role was to gather bush food, while the elderly people stayed in the family camp and cared for the children. Each knew his own place in the social order. As a result of the imposition of Christianity, and with the government's financial support, there has been a shift in the social status of women who no longer need to be subservient, although most of the women tend to consider their husbands to be the 'boss'.

Currently, many of the middle-aged Lardil, especially the women, continue to be active in the Mission church. The Christian teachings and beliefs are revealed in their conversation, and in some aspects of their behaviour. However, most of the younger Lardil women and the Kaiadilt are much less involved in the church. The middle-aged women are troubled by this lessening of interest in Christianity.

The Presbyterian Mission Board is attempting to have some of the church elders trained as lay ministers, and is helping them to develop a service which combines traditional beliefs and customs with the Christian service. How much the younger Lardil will be involved in this effort is problematical. The socially excluded Kaiadilt are not likely to become intrigued by this movement.

The social institution of marriage, and of the monogamous nuclear family, is losing importance among the younger people; although most of the women, at least verbally, wish for a husband. Assisted by the economic patronage, the women are able to cope with the inclusion of young children into the extended families, frequently without assistance from the biological fathers.

In the traditional culture, early childhood training did not emphasize stepping outside the family group for individual, independent achievement. The early Mission was authoritarian, and encouraged compliance and conformity rather than individuality and initiative. At the present time some individuals are obtaining a measure of recognition and success, such as the dance groups and the artists, usually as a result of activities which bring them into contact with greater Australia. However, there is evidence of jealousy on the part of those who are not as fortunate. A few of the children of women who originally came from the mainland are viewed as having better jobs, on or off the island. These women are accused of 'pushing' their children. As an expression of jealousy, although these mothers have lived most of their lives on the island, they are taunted with accusations of being 'half-white' or with thinking they are 'so smart' because they are 'mainlanders'.

Elsie feels she is not liked. A plausible explanation mentioned earlier is that many are jealous because Elsie expresses her opinions and commands respect for her ideas. Dick's success as a painter and writer in the greater Australian community is also resented. When he attempts to organize activities on the island, his efforts are frequently met with passive resistance. It is dangerous to strive. One may not be liked if he steps out of the group and improves his status. This, perhaps, accounts for the lack of motivation for achievement among the children in the secondary schools. The Manager reported that many of the youngsters who early show good academic achievement suddenly lose all interest in school when they reach pubescence, as if they 'turn off' their ability to learn. He postulated that academic superiority is not acceptable, as it makes one stand out from the group. This is in agreement with Watts, the leading authority concerned with Aboriginal education, who stated, 'The Aboriginal child who succeeds places himself in a minority group within his own culture'.[7]

We have seen that kinship customs continue to be important in the Islanders' lives. These, in part, connote certain social obligations. One's extended kinship family is expected to share food or whatever is needed, although there is evidence that there are now limitations to this type of generosity. Various of the traditional practices serve to insure such co-operation and support. The *junge*, or navel cord custom, presupposes that the children so honoured will look after their older relatives when they become adults. In part, the inter-family strife that occurs when a wrong-head marriage is contemplated is based on the fear that a daughter-in-law or son-in-law of such a marriage will not be as dutiful, helpful, and generous as could be expected of one in a right-head union.

In summary, the social changes initiated by the institution of the Mission have augmented the social status of the women, but have diminished the power of the men. The social institution of marriage is weakening. Drinking and gambling have been introduced by contact with white man's society. The social obligation of the kinship system, which implies dependency on the extended family structure, continues but shows signs of disruption. The early Mission encouraged compliance and dependence. Changing one's social status by stepping out for greater achievement was not adaptive in the pre-Mission and early Mission days. The beginning achievement and increased social status of some of the Islanders now produces some inter-family conflict and potential rejection by the community. One may be excluded from one's own group as well as from the dominant society.

Political Influences. The Islanders have been under the control of the Mission and of various agencies of the Queensland government, which have provided them with protection and guidance as well as money. Except for several brief periods, the Reserve has been under the direction of only two missionaries, who were in residence for extended

periods of time. The first, the Reverend R. Wilson, was in charge
during the days of the dormitory. As nearly as can be ascertained, not
only was he restrictive and authoritarian, but he regarded the Lardil
people as children, and treated them as such. In contrast, the Reverend
Douglas Belcher attempted to relate to them as adults.

Mr Belcher, in an effort to encourage responsibility, control, and
some autonomy in the Islanders, promoted the development of the
village Council and employed local men as police. In spite of his efforts
to encourage self-determination, the people repeatedly turned to Mr
Belcher to arbitrate their disputes, and the Council depended on him
for guidance and decision-making.

In 1973, in addition to the manager, accountant, nursing sisters, and
teachers, all the supervisory personnel were white. The latter included
the store manager, stenographer, cattle manager, mechanic, electrician,
and builder. The handcraft shop was the only operation of which the
management had been assumed by the Aborigines.

In the early seventies there was a growing feeling throughout
Australia that the official government policy of 'assimilation' would not
work; and that it should be replaced by a policy loosely defined but
widely known as 'self-determination'. With this in mind, The Mission
Board first approached the Islanders in late 1970 with the idea that the
people should take over the administration of the island. It was at that
time that Elsie said, 'They (the Aborigines) think it too hard to live like
white man; they would rather live the simple life they are now living.
They think it a bit hard, it frightens them.' She further expressed the
opinion that any development on the island would only be successful if
under the close supervision of white people.

However, when I returned to Mornington three years later, the legal
papers for the incorporation of the island as an independent community
were ready for signing. It would then be up to the new Board of
Directors of the Corporation to decide whether or not they wanted to
employ white advisers for overall administration, as well as for
supervision of the store and other activities.

Although the actual transfer was not to become effective until eight
months hence, almost every person expressed great concern about this
anticipated political move that would put them in control. As reported
in the biographical material, the causes verbalized for their anxieties
varied. Elsie did not think that they would have the knowledge to
manage such practical affairs as ordering supplies, keeping records, or
operating the wireless. Other individuals were more concerned about
the current stealing, drinking, and gambling, and diminution of church
attendance. They felt these activities, which they considered deviant,
would only become worse with the Mission withdrawal. They feared

that law and order might break down completely and if it did the school teachers and nursing sisters might leave.

Another area of concern centred around the influence of kinship. Many felt that those in power would favour their relatives with the better paying jobs and other types of favouritism. It was known that, even before incorporation, some of the police had overlooked infractions, such as stealing, when the guilty party was one of their kin. A further example mentioned was that, in the beer canteen, some of those selling the beer saw to it that their relatives got more than the allotted number of cans.

The only statement concerning the anticipated incorporation that showed any positive attitude was made by one of the young women who said, 'I'm on the Board of Directors; I've got to believe it will work.'

Those most concerned were the younger Kaiadilt. They feared being discriminated against, in that they would be given no share of the power and no opportunity for paying jobs. They anticipated that the shift in administration might produce a situation so unfavourable for them that they would be compelled to leave the island.

The attitude of the Mission Board is that its aim is to help people to help themselves. Another way of looking at the proposed change was expressed by a member of the Mission staff who said, 'At some time parents need to let their children go and take responsibility for themselves.' The question in the minds of the people seems to be, 'Do we have the knowledge and controls to be able to take responsibility for directing ourselves and the affairs of our island?' It is to be remembered that the people had neither been seeking freedom from the Mission nor self-government. There were no militant Aborigines on Mornington. The people had expected their affairs to be guided and controlled by the agencies of the Mission and the government, and had adjusted to this passive attitude. They now have many doubts about the political shift that will require a more active, self-reliant mode of life.

Psychological Factors and Adaptation

For the Mornington Islanders, the political change with which they will soon be confronted has been described. While this anticipated change was perceived by the people as threatening, it is not as radical as if two divergent cultural systems were confronting each other with great rapidity in all environmental aspects for the first time.

Spindler used the term 'reactive movements' to indicate exaggerated forms of ordinary response to change.[8] Other anthropologists have labelled such responses as reformulative, nativistic, revitalizing, or reaffirmative. Spindler saw reactive movements to change as having two common features: the search for identity, and the attempt to re-establish cognitive control. From his point of view these features were most important to a people when faced with radical change, especially when divergent cultural systems confront each other.

As Spindler used the term, 'Identity . . . is composed in part of one's own image of self, in part of one's perception of others' estimates, in part of the rationalization of discrepancies between the two.'[9] The search for identity is central to ego psychology.

Reaffirmation of their Identity as Aborigines. In ego psychology, the term identity is used to describe 'a conscious sense of one's individual uniqueness, as an unconscious striving for a continuity of experience, and as his solidarity with a group's ideals.'[10] The individual's identity is idiosyncratic and is based on his own particular wishes, thoughts, and memories. A group shares a collective identity insofar as its members have congruent images and perceptions. Being a member of a group is part of the individual's self-image. Individual and group identity as well as the unconscious wish for continuity of experiences can be succinctly illustrated by Elsie's self-affirmation, 'I am Elsie Roughsey, a Lardil Aborigine of Mornington Island. I am proud to be an Aborigine.'

Because of the isolation of the island, the only white people with whom the indigenous residents have daily contact are the staff of the Mission. They see Western culture as portrayed in the films which are shown several times a week. These are apt to be travelogues, educational, or religious films. Radios provide a source of music; however, news or other types of programmes appear to hold little interest.

Those Islanders who travel to the mainland for work or holiday are exposed to European ways. What most impresses the women who have visited the towns and cities is the way people dress, and especially that everyone wears shoes. Those who spend extended periods away are reported to quickly drop their Western cultural trappings and to mesh into the island customs upon their return.

The concepts of assimilation and integration with the greater Australian society do not particularly occupy the people's thinking. However, there are a number of areas where they indicate growing awareness that they are Aborigines who want to maintain or reaffirm their identity as such. After their dormitory years, which had interrupted the natural transmission of their native culture, many actively sought to learn the myths, legends and practices of their Lardil ancestors. We have seen how such traditional beliefs as sorcery and *malgri* continue to influence their thinking. The Lardil corroboree dance groups have received acclaim from the greater Australian society, which no doubt has motivated them to maintain and improve this form of artistic expression. This recognition has made the dancers aware that they have something special to offer as Aborigines. No doubt this has increased their self-esteem as a group. A few, but especially Dick Roughsey, move in some important Australian circles, either through their accomplishments as artists, or as contributors of Aboriginal tradition to national councils or committees.

The importance of kinship traditions is woven throughout their lives, in spite of the looseness in which it is maintained. An example of how this concept may be gaining interest and prestige in the young is illustrated by the following. I asked a dormitory-reared woman whether her daughter had a right-head marriage. She thought for a moment and then replied, 'No, but I'm pleased with my son-in-law. He's a more reliable worker and husband than I had thought he would be.' During a rather long and casual conversation with this young man, he related that his is a right-head marriage. I did not press him for the details of this, as it seemed obvious that it was important to him to present his marriage as upholding Aboriginal tradition.

Perhaps the strongest indication of the Lardil (or those raised and married into the group) to maintain their identity as Aborigines is revealed in the statements of a number of the women that they hoped that their daughters would marry dark-skinned men, not white men. Catherine Elong would be disappointed if her daughter, Ida, disowned her Aboriginal background and passed into white society. Of course, she would be disowning her mother at the same time, and Catherine is pleased that she, herself, has chosen to remain an Aborigine.

The reaffirmation of the Aboriginal identity of the Lardil may be compared to Linton's concept of nativistic movements, which he defined as 'any conscious, organized attempt on the part of a society's members to revive or perpetuate selected aspects of its culture'.[11] The Lardil have and are reviving and perpetuating aspects that have both magical and rational elements. The reaffirmation of the Lardil identity is not so much the result of conflict between dominant and inferior groups, or social disorganization; rather, it is the result of characteristics in their cultural heritage that make them unique as a people. In addition, there are many aspects that are personally satisfying.

The Kaiadilt are not in as favourable a situation. In addition to extreme social disintegration on Bentinck, they are considered inferior by the dominant Lardil and fear for their future if the Lardil control the island administration. Among the Kaiadilt, there is group cohesion for mutual security and some sense of worth in considering themselves to be reliable workers, at least in routine or menial tasks. However, this small, excluded group has not attained any status on Mornington and does not have the type of artistic expression (handcraft techniques, painting or dance) that would appear to, and get acclaim from, white Australians. While there is potential within individual members for responsibility and reliability, their marginal position on the island and lack of recognition from without does not promote pride in their identity as Kaiadilt Aborigines. Those few people, who learn to know some of the Kaiadilt in a more than superficial way, feel respect for them.

The Cognitive Process and Control. Spindler, in his model for psychocultural adaptation, postulated that the ability to establish cognitive control is an important factor in the psychology of an individual when he and his group are confronted with a divergent cultural system. He defined the cognitive process as 'the way a person views, sorts, and synthesizes the things and events believed to exist in the world, in order to produce a relevant response'.[12]

Prior to the arrival of the Mission staff, the people of Mornington had a very different conception of his world and of natural events. They made no distinction between man and natural species, as revealed in Dick Roughsey's account of the rainbow serpent and a mob of people: the stingray, the bluefish, the seagull . . . and others.[13] Time was limitless and intimately related to their mythical ancestors.[14] More immediate time was governed by the seasons and what natural foods were available. Their own particular traditional culture informed their lives in order to produce a relevant response.

However, during the past sixty years Western concepts of time and other events in the world have been imposed on them. If the Mornington people are going to be responsible for the administration of their island, this will demand even more Western styles of organization. Further changes will be necessary in their cognitive functioning.

I believe that the factors contributing to the cognitive process may be better understood by using some of the concepts of ego psychology. The ego is defined as the part of the psychic apparatus that mediates between a person's intra-psychic reality and external reality. The functions of the ego are numerous; those to be mentioned here deal with some of the important aspects of the cognitive process.

It is evident that the Lardil and the younger Kaiadilt have been able to master such ego functions as acquiring a second language, memory, reading, and thinking. We have seen how they have been able to integrate certain beliefs from two divergent cultures (Aboriginal and Western) without much evidence of personal conflict.

Other aspects of ego function are important in the cognitive process. Among the most basic is the ability to follow simple routines with some adherence to time. As mentioned earlier, Western and traditional

Aboriginal concepts of time are vastly different. However, those routines firmly established by the Mission, such as store hours to buy food and clothing, time to receive allotment money, or to sell their handcraft, are to a great extent followed by the people. However, if a new routine requiring individual initiative is expected, such as taking a medicine at stated times, this may not be followed with any regularity. In the first instances the routines were probably more readily established by the immediacy of reward, which provided positive reinforcement for conforming behaviour. In the case of taking medicine, the immediate reinforcement might be negative and the resulting cure delayed. The delay of gratification is an important ego function.

Another aspect of the ego is the ability to tolerate reasonable frustration. What is reasonable in reference to frustration also depends on the culture and the Aborigines have been thwarted many times. However, in the past, when the slightest ache or pain was felt by adults or by their children, the attention of the nursing sister was almost immediately sought, whether it be midday or midnight. Whenever the nurses made any attempt to curtail responding, they were met with petulant anger. By 1973, a new nursing staff had set limits which the Islanders had learned to accept. Will the people be able to impose, accept, and integrate additional limits set by their own group?

The regulation and control of emotion mediated by the ego is important for the cognitive process. The manner in which the Islanders deal with anger and display aggression has been revealed in many of the biographies of the women. When displeasure or anger is aroused in one as the result of the behaviour of another, it is typical to avoid confronting the offending individual. Elsie's ability to confront her children with their delinquent behaviour is a good example of this. Pearl Yates did not want her children to think that she might be 'meddling in their affairs'. One does not reprimand another person's children for destructive behaviour for fear of arousing anger. Standing up for one's self or one's children, such as Rose Johns did, earned her the reputation of being a 'fighter'; and that is not socially acceptable. If a request is made of another, instead of being told no, the request may simply not be fulfilled. Possibly the early Mission training, which frowned on aggression, may have largely contributed to this avoidance behaviour. Will the potential island leaders be able to be more assertive in confronting their own people (or the government) to obtain their goals?

In contrast are the outbreaks of violence that intermittently erupt in the village. In all probability, this violence is a break-through of aggression when anger can no longer be suppressed or avoided. The fights usually start with a small disagreement, not infrequently over the behaviour of children, and may spread from verbal insults between the mothers of the offending children to the various kinship groups, who then may resort to the use of sticks and boomerangs. An older, respected person may be able to intervene. The local police and the Mission manager may have success in stopping the violence; however, at times it is necessary to call police from the mainland. The fighting has become more common with the availability of beer and the illegal hard liquor.

Being able to delay immediate gratification for future gain had not been a necessary part of the Aboriginal life-style. Prior to the Mission, the people had adapted to the hunting and gathering as the environment provided. They did not store supplies, but ate their food and when hungry sought more. With their knowledge of what foods were available at any particular season, they did not worry about tomorrow.[15] During their residence in the dormitory, food and shelter were provided. After leaving the dormitory, many of the men and some of the women would intermittently leave the island to earn money to support themselves and their families. A few continue to do so.

In recent years, the increasing government allotments have provided most of the necessities of life and some luxuries, such as fibreglass boats with outboard motors. It is evident that most of their current basic dependency needs are met and that they primarily 'live for today'. However, a few who have paying jobs 'save for tomorrow' for such things as the purchase of a refrigerator or for a trip to the mainland. Delay for future gain has been part of the ego operation for some.

There may be a marked hiatus between the inception of an idea and the formulation and execution of plans. For example, although Elsie had expected me to stay with her on my return visit, she did not get around to making the necessary changes in her household to accommodate Nancy Waxler and me until our arrival. There is a disinclination to plan ahead, to have food and other necessities available. This again may reveal that a different time sense continues to operate. The absence of formulating plans is most striking when a group activity is to take place. If the Womens Group of the Church were to decide to have a social function, it would come about only if a member of the Mission group were to take over the direction.

Ingenuity and resourcefulness in developing new ideas and methods is a high-order ego function necessary in Western culture. In various ways the Aborigines followed the ways of their ancestors. In our 'rock oystering' expedition, the women broke the shells loose from the rocks with stones, and gouged out the oysters with their fingers. They were employing a time-honoured approach. I was the only one who seemed aware that this was an inefficient way to collect rock oysters. While the men have fibreglass boats with high powered outboard motors, they hunt and fish with spears. In another instance, Mrs Vines wished for some method to hang up her freshly ironed clothes. Hangers were available from the clothing store. She was amazed at my simple suggestion that a broom handle could be utilized as a rod for the hangers.

Some of the various functions of the ego that give an individual the capacity to unite, organize, and bind together various drives and tendencies so that he can feel, think, and act in an organized and directed manner have been discussed. These are facets of the cognitive process that allow for cognitive control, which Spindler rightly maintains is a vital part of psychocultural adaptation to change. The Islanders in order to adapt to the demands of their new political environment for self-government and self-administration of their own socioeconomic affairs will need to apply Western-type cognitive modes.

Certainly the people, themselves, doubt their readiness for the task. They view the change less as an opportunity than as a threat. Their anxiety reflects some awareness that the cognitive control essential for change will be difficult for them. Of course, some readers may want to explain the anxiety of the people as reflecting a natural resistance to any change in what is a familiar life-style.

If we consider the four basic components in adaptation to the human environment listed by Mitscherlich,[16] we might say these Aborigines seem to have negotiated the first two: passive adaptation to existing conditions, and some control of their impulses to the outside world. However, they have not achieved the other two components: he lists active adaptation by shaping their own environment, and taking initiative for shaping their own behaviour.

Another approach to understanding the problems facing the Mornington Islanders in their current transitional phase of psychocultural adaptation is suggested by Brody's concept of 'cultural exclusion'.[17] Brody identified four elements of culture that affect the individual who is denied full participation in the dominant society. Two of these elements are clearly pertinent to these Aborigines: 'There is less free-choice and self-determination . . . Individual gain through collective behaviour is (stifled) by others.'[18] We have seen that individual success experienced by some of the Islanders aroused hostility in members of their own community. Others limited their potential for accomplishment so as not to feel like a minority in their own group. Thus, the danger of isolation by their group for having made individual gains is probably as potent a stifling factor for the Mornington people as is suppression by the dominant society. Clearly there are elements affecting the subordinate individual that do not originate exclusively in the dominant culture.

Brody's third and fourth elements affecting the subordinate individual are that 'he is excluded from a range of achievement-oriented behaviours because of his lack of . . . experiences important to the development of incentive. Lastly, there is the relative lack of specific cultural symbols that allow for richness, continuity, and integration of experiences. This produces fewer opportunities for consummatory experiences because fewer rewards are available to him for productive effort . . . as a result he has a constricted range of ego defensive and adaptive techniques.'[19] Although the Mornington Island people have had a limited range of ego adaptive techniques, they do not lack cultural features that provide some richness and continuity of experience.

As Brody aptly paraphrased Erikson, 'Ego identity gains real strength only from the whole-hearted and constant recognition of achievement that has meaning to the culture.'[20] In the islanders' transition toward self-government, there is potential for development of greater self-esteem and strength in their identity as Aborigines. There is the possibility of greater amalgamation of some of the traditional beliefs and practices with the teachings of the Mission and Western culture. Only time will tell if this will promote changes that will provide individual and group recognition and satisfaction sufficient to allow for a different level of psychocultural adaptation.

In any event, the current problem for the Mornington Islanders cannot be better expressed than by Hartmann's observation, 'man's environment is moulded increasingly by himself. Thus, the crucial adaptation man has to make is to the social structure, and his collaboration in building it.'[21]

Notes

1. Burness E. Moore and Bernard D. Fine, *A Glossary of Psychoanalytic Terms and Concepts.* New York, American Psychoanalytic Association, 1967, p. 12.
2. Heinz Hartmann, *Ego Psychology and the Problem of Adaptation.* New York, International Universities Press, Inc., 1958.
3. George O. Spindler, 'Psychocultural Adaptation', in *The Study of Personality: An Interdisciplinary Appraisal,* Edward Norbeck, Douglas Price-Williams and William McCord (eds). New York, Holt, Rinehart and Winston, Inc., 1968, pp. 326-347.
4. Heinz Hartmann, *Ego Psychology.* op. cit. pp. 24-26.
5. George O. Spindler, *The Study of Personality,* op. cit. p. 326.
6. David Omar Born, 'Psychological Adaptation and Development Under Acculturative Stress', *Social Science and Medicine* 3, 1970, pp. 538-539.
7. B. H. Watts, 'Personality Factors in the Academic Success of Adolescent Girls', in *The Psychology of Aboriginal Australians,* G. E. Kearney, P. R. de Lacey and G. R. Davidson (eds). Sydney, John Wiley and Sons Australasia, 1973, p. 284.

8.   Spindler, op. cit. pp. 332-335.
9.   ibid., p. 336.
10. Erik H. Erikson, *Identity, Youth and Crisis.* New York, W. W. Horton & Co., 1968, p. 208.
11. Ralph Linton, 'Nativistic Movements', *American Anthropologist,* 45, 1943, p. 230.
12. Spindler, op. cit. p. 338.
13. See Chapter 2.
14. Roughsey, op. cit. p. 20.
15. See Roughsey, op. cit. pp. 41-48, for description of the varied bush and seafoods available and the method for obtaining them.
16. Alexander Mitscheslich, *Society Without the Father.* New York, Harcourt, Brace and World, Inc., 1969, p. 6.
17. Eugene B. Brody, 'Cultural Exclusion, Character and Illness', *American Journal of Psychiatry,* Vol. 122, 1966, pp. 852-858.
18. ibid., p. 854.
19. ibid.
20. ibid., p. 855.
21. Hartmann, *Ego Psychology,* op. cit. p. 31.

Addendum
Legal Status of Mornington Island, July 1974

It has been the aim of the Board of Ecumenical Missions and Relations of the Presbyterian Church of Australia to enable the Aboriginal communities under their jurisdiction to achieve the responsibility for administrating their own communities as soon as possible. Incorporation, which has allowed autonomy for the Aboriginal communities formerly under control of the Mission Board, has been successfully completed in Western Australia and South Australia.

However, with the passage of the Queensland Aborigines Act of 1971, and the accompanying Aborigines Regulations of 1972 passed by the Parliament of Queensland, it has not been possible to complete the incorporation as had been planned by the Board of Missions and the Mornington Island community. Under the Act, the Manager of the Mission must continue to have the overriding authority. It is only possible to transfer decision-making within certain areas of enterprise. For that reason, as of July 1 1974, two companies had been formed.

The first, Gunana-Manda[1] Incorporated Pty, Ltd which has a board of fifteen directors, including five from the Council, is responsible for all enterprises such as the general store, clothing store, handcraft, cattle, tourism, and in the future, fishing or any other industry which may be established.

The second company, Gunana-Manda Housing Corporation Pty, Ltd, has been set up to enable financial assistance from the Commonwealth Government to be given directly to the community rather than following the former policy of giving money through some agency, such as a mission. This Housing Corporation will be responsible for all future building erection, alteration, and maintenance.

This means that the community has the final say in the areas mentioned. Through the companies, the people have the right to hire and fire Advisers whom they may wish to appoint to assist them.

At a general meeting the community unanimously decided to continue the Mission staff as Advisers to the various enterprises, so that the general store, clothing store and cattle operation are under the same staff as they were prior to the formation of Gunana-Manda Company.

The Manager and other staff continue as Mission Board appointees and have the final say over administration, public works, and other activities not under the areas of enterprise. As a result there have been no staff changes attributable to Incorporation.

I am endebted to Mr A. M. Gibson, Manager, for the above information.

Notes

1. 'Gunana' the Lardil name for Mornington Island, 'Manda' signifies 'people of'.

References

Barnes, John. 'Some Ethical Problems in Modern Field Work.' *British Journal of Sociology* 14, 1963, 118-34.

Berndt, Ronald M., and Berndt, Catherine H. *Sexual Behaviour in Western Arnhem Land.* New York, Wenner-Gren Foundation for Anthropological Research, 1951.

Born, David Omar. 'Psychological Adaptation and Development Under Acculturative Stress.' *Social Science and Medicine* 3, 1970, 529-47.

Brody, Eugene B. 'Cultural Exclusion, Character and Illness.' *American Journal of Psychiatry* 122, 1966, 852-58.

Calhoun, John B. 'Plight of the Ik and Kaiadilt is seen as a chilling possible end for Man.' *Smithsonian* 3, 1972, 27-32.

Cawte, John. *Cruel, Poor and Brutal Nations.* Honolulu, University Press of Hawaii, 1972.

Cawte, John. *Medicine is the Law.* Honolulu, University Press of Hawaii, 1974.

Elkin, A. P. *The Australian Aborigines.* Garden City, New York, Doubleday & Co., 1964.

Festinger, Leon. *A Theory of Cognitive Dissonance.* Stanford, California, Stanford University Press, 1957.

Gale, Fay, ed. *Woman's Role in Aboriginal Society.* Australian Aboriginal Studies, No. 36. Australian Institute of Aboriginal Studies, Canberra. 1970.

Goodale, Jane. *Tiwi Wives.* Seattle, University of Washington Press, 1971.

Gottschalk, Louis; Kluckhohn, Clyde and Angell, Robert. *The Use of Personal Document in History, Anthropology and Sociology.* New York, Social Science Research Council Bulletin 53, 1945.

Hart, C. W. M., and Pilling, Arnold. *The Tiwi of North Australia.* New York, Holt, Rinehart and Winston, 1960.

Hartmann, Heinz. *Ego Pscychology and the Problem of Adaptation.* New York, International Universities Press, 1958.

Howard, Richard B. Queensland Aboriginals, Chief Protector. Report in *Queensland Parliamentary Papers,* Vol. 2, 1909, pp. 970-3.

Huffer, Virginia. 'Australian Aborigine: Transition in Family Grouping.' *Family Process* 12, 1973, 303-315.

Hughes, Charles C. 'Life History in Cross-cultural Psychiatric Research.' In *Approaches to Cross-cultural Psychiatry.* Edited by J. N. Murphy and A. H. Leighton. Ithaca, Cornell University Press, 1966, pp. 285-328.